Château Pichon-Longueville Comtesse de Lalande

A Passion for Wine

Graphic Design : Lorette Mayon
Translation : Miranda Richmond-Mouillot and Jennifer Cohen

David Haziot
With the participation of May-Eliane de Lencquesaing
Preface and tasting notes by Serena Sutcliffe

Photography by Anne Garde • Portrait recreations by François Baranger

CHÂTEAU PICHON-LONGUEVILLE COMTESSE DE LALANDE

A Passion for Wine

**Éditions
de La Martinière**

TABLE OF CONTENTS

• Preface by Serena Sutcliffe.. 6

• "An Unforgettable Wine"... 9

• The Origins of Winegrowing in the Médoc 11

• The Founders 13

Pierre Rauzan 13

Bernard de Pichon 29

• Ladies of the Vine 35

• Baron Joseph (1760-1849) 47

• Sophie and Virginie
Founders of Pichon-Lalande (1856) 63

Sophie, Painter and Romantic (1785-1858) 63

Virginie, Comtesse de Lalande (1798-1882) 83

• The Age of Crisis and Disease 97

• The Era of Great Courage
Louis and Edouard Miailhe 111

• A New Dimension
May-Eliane and Hervé de Lencquesaing 139

• Conclusion 189

• Appendices

Pichon-Longueville Family Tree.. 190

Lalande and Lacroix Family Tree.. 192

The Miailhes: A great Bordeaux Wine Family.. 194

Descendants of Edouard Miailhe

and Anglo-Philippine ancestry of his wife, Victoria Desbarats 196

Pichon-Longueville Comtesse de Lalande • Tasting notes

by Serena Sutcliffe 198

Bibliography 203

Acknowledgements... 207

PREFACE

Reading this book resembles having a glass of very good wine, preferably Pichon Lalande. It is stimulating, it uplifts and it unfolds in fascinating fashion. In fact, the components that make up both the contents of a book and of a wine have certain similarities. Both should have character, individuality, layers and dimension if they are not to be simplistic and facsimiles of other productions. The blend is also important, just as it is in a top wine from the Médoc such as Pichon, where the proportions of four grape varieties are magically juggled to create a harmonious whole. In this book, the "assemblage" is riveting, combining the astonishing archives miraculously discovered in the attics of Pichon by May-Eliane de Lencquesaing and her own, vibrant memories. It is our good fortune that May-Eliane, this vital link in the chain, has prodigious powers of recall and, when this is added to the meticulous research of David Haziot, the result keeps us glued to the page.

There are many elements throughout this history of one of France's greatest wines that are as applicable today as they were centuries ago. Absolute respect for the land and its gifts is almost a prerequisite. The value of continuity is immediately apparent, as is the need for real application and hard work if one wishes to produce a wine of enduring quality. Investment, both personal and financial, is vital. There is so much that has not changed. The vagaries of climate are still with us, whether it is an excess of heat (in 1893, the harvest began on 17 August with a temperature of 46 degrees, more extreme than in 2003!) or of rain, or the constant combat against the ravages of disease. The development of the use of sulphur to preserve wine appears much earlier than we might have thought, precisely at the insistence of Pierre Rauzan towards the end of the 17th century. The Médoc classification of 1855 is always in our minds, but here we see all the "classements" that went before it. Understanding how the wine trade works and going with the tides of the time are primordial if a property is to remain financially viable for hundreds of years – the parallel trading of cod and wine was as necessary in the

17th century as is world-wide promotion of one's château in the 21st. Fraud and authenticity were issues in the 19th century, as they are now, with constant vigilance the sole cure.

A very clear idea of what is required in order to run a great wine property emerges from this book. Lucidity of direction is an asset that is shared by all those who owned, managed, even coaxed Pichon to perfection. Baron Joseph de Pichon-Longueville epitomises resilience in the face of enormous challenges, which included both the Revolution and the Terror – against this background he succeeded in ushering his property to the ranks of a second growth, no mean feat. He also left the estate to his four surviving children, with Virginie the most dynamic among them, managing the land of all three sisters and building the château, *chai* and *cuvier* of Pichon-Lalande. It is perhaps the "luck of the draw" that, over the centuries, this particular great Bordeaux *cru* has had a series of owners who have been imbued by a real passion for wine.

One can almost trace the history of Pichon Lalande by looking at the portraits and paintings at the château itself, although I have long thought that the image that is missing is that of May-Eliane de Lencquesaing who, from 1978 to 2007, has been the life-force of this most inspiring of Bordeaux's great *crus*. No one could have been a more worthy successor to Virginie, La Comtesse de Lalande, and to her father and uncle, Edouard and Louis Miailhe. Pichon now enters new, family ownership, with all colours flying. It is a phenomenal responsibility, with myriad attention to detail and aptitude for taking the right decisions as important today as they were when mildew stalked the vineyards and wars threatened the principal client markets.

The story of Pichon Lalande is of vicissitudes and victories, of human foibles and brilliance, of determination and devotion. Ultimately, it is also the story of Bordeaux and, thus, of France.

Serena Sutcliffe

Master of Wine, director of Sotheby's international wine department,
author of numerous books about wine.

"An Unforgettable Wine"

The life's dream of Virginie de Pichon-Longueville, Comtesse de Lalande, was to make an "unforgettable wine." The Médoc's *deuxième grand cru classé* bears her name, and has indeed been characterized as "irresistible"* – in certain years it surpasses all other wines.

Structured and velvety, it has all the elegance of the great Médoc wines, with no excess of voluptuousness or roundness. It is a wine that lingers cleanly in the mouth, as if it were giving you permission to savor it from a distance, to reflect freely on its taste; it gives as much pleasure to the spirit as it does to the senses.

The *cru*'s story merits telling. It shares its history with its brother, Pichon-Longueville Baron, until 1850, when it takes a dramatically different turn.

The history of Pichon-Longueville Comtesse de Lalande is tied to the very origins of the Médoc winemaking tradition. It winds through the legacy of the great family of Pichon-Longueville, who tinged it with drama and romance. It is the history of France itself, in its darkest and brightest hours. And it counts at least as many women as it does men in its ranks.

These days, it is no longer rare to see a woman at the head of a *grand cru*. Pichon-Longueville, however, was a pioneer in the field. From the very beginning, and then in the days following the division of the two châteaux, it has nearly always been run by women. Seven women have presided over its destiny, three of them for over a quarter century each. Nine men have filled the same role, some for fewer than ten years, some for only two. It should be noted that this strong feminine presence did nothing to eclipse the remarkable men who made the *cru* what it is today, starting with its founder, Pierre Rauzan; indeed, a real balance exists between the two.

Given this succession of often surprising personalities (such enterprises, after all, call for great strength of character), it seemed logical to write this history as a kind of portrait gallery. Each portrait varies depending on the documentation available. What follows is the history of Pichon-Longueville, and the history of Pichon-Longueville Comtesse de Lalande, seen through the eyes of the men and women who built it over three centuries. Without, of course, overlooking the vines, barrels, prices, and classifications that gave the *cru* its unique character, we will examine the lives that brought it to greater and greater heights, until it became what it is today.

* Nuikki, *Drinking History, Stories from Wines and Vintages (1870-1970)*.

THE ORIGINS OF WINEGROWING IN THE MEDOC

The Médoc, one of the world's most beautiful wine regions, was discovered late. Nothing about the desolate peninsula, isolated between river and sky, sea and rain, seemed to destine it for its fate. To the west lay infertile, sandy terrain described in unsparing terms by writers of old; to the east, nothing of any note grew from the rocky hillsides along the Gironde River. Pauillac and Beychevelle were originally only stopovers for ships awaiting the tide to carry them to Bordeaux or to the high seas. Wine had not yet reached the Médoc, but was abundant further upstream, around Bordeaux, which by 1310 was exporting 900,000 hecto-liters (24 million gallons) annually, a staggering figure considering contemporary resources, the city's size, and the ships available. Bordeaux's merchant class did all it could to convince Britain and Northern Europe that Bordeaux wines were the finest available. Since the Middle Ages, entire fleets had sailed north carrying them.

Since no preservation techniques yet existed, these were young wines. The largest shipments went out before Christmas, as wines produced within the year began turning by Easter. Sulfur wicks, whose combustion sterilizes the wood inside closed barrels before filling, would not be introduced until the turn of the 18th century. As they had since antiquity, people drank either *vins cuits* or young, fruity wines, like Beaujolais Nouveaux.

And what of the Médoc at that time? Quite simply, nearly nothing: according to one author, the landscape was barren except for the occasional sickly sheep in search of a tuft of grass. Around the villages, peasants labored to coax a few cabbages from the rocky ground. With no enology, geomorphology, chemistry, ampelography, or aerial photography, how did anyone discover that growing wine grapes in this hostile land would produce such an exquisite perfume? Grapes were already grown for sacramental wine across France, as far as Lille. The Médoc was no exception: abbeys like Vertheuil and Ordonnac produced their own wines.

How and to whom did the idea of growing grapes for wine occur? The best answer is that it emerged gradually. The history of these *terroirs* is one of an encounter between the mysterious powers of man over the sacred vines, and the palates of those who drank the wines they produced. Men and women, armed with little more than their minds, their notes, and the knowledge of generations past – those Châteaubriand called "the dusty family of the dead,"* – slowly perfected the region's wines. A wine was good, or not, could be better, was easier to sell in distant countries. Producers were eager to meet the demands of the latter's high paying customers.

The great Bordeaux wines were the work of French – more specifically, Gascon – palates, but also of English ones. The *entente cordiale* has deep roots: though France and England were often at war, London's affection for Bordeaux wines rarely wavered.

But who first truly understood the potential of Médoc wines? Does this discoverer have a name? Perhaps.

Thanks to historical enology, a surprising, long-neglected figure emerges from the fog of history. No one can say whether he really was the first, but he was certainly among the first. Even if he did not himself discover Médoc wines, his actions lead us to believe that he was the first to measure their true potential – or even to be able to do so. His name was Pierre Rauzan; he was a member of the Bordeaux merchant class. In addition to establishing a vineyard in his own name, he founded what would become Pichon-Longueville.

* Alexander Teixeira de Mattos (trans.), *The Memoirs of François René Vicomte de Chateaubriand.* London: Freemantle, 1902.

THE FOUNDERS

This story begins with two men, Pierre Rauzan and Bernard de Pichon. The former created the estate, and the actions of the latter brought renown to the Pichon-Longueville family. What follows is the story of a great wine, the land, and the men – and women – who made it what it is.

At the time of Louis XIV, Pierre Rauzan and Bernard de Pichon were among Bordeaux's most prominent figures. Pierre Rauzan was of bourgeois origin, and Bernard de Pichon was a member of the pre-Revolutionary *parlement* – a merchant and a magistrate. Pierre Rauzan's daughter, Thérèse Rauzan, married Bernard de Pichon's youngest son, Jacques-François de Pichon. This marriage produced a great wine, now divided between two facing châteaux: Pichon-Longueville Baron and Pichon-Longueville Comtesse. One might call them the "gentlemen's château" and the "ladies' château," and not entirely in jest; it is the way things were, a reminder of the eternal duality of our condition.

Pierre Rauzan and Bernard de Pichon had one thing in common: they both emerged victorious from the Fronde, the crisis that shook France a century and a half before the Revolution.

PIERRE RAUZAN

A force of nature

Pierre Rauzan – or, more precisely, Pierre Desmesures, known as Rauzan – was born around 1620 at the very latest, perhaps a few years earlier.* It would seem that he came from the Rauzan domain in the Entre-Deux-Mers. Little by little, a series of official acts shows his patronymic disappear and the name of his village emerge, and before long, he was simply known as Pierre Rauzan, or "the sire [*sieur*] Rauzan." Rauzan grew wealthy and purchased the noble house of Gassie; his children adopted the noble article, calling themselves "de Rauzan."

* René Pijassou, *Château Rauzan-Ségla, la naissance d'un grand cru classé*, Paris, Éditions de La Martinière, 2004. This chapter offers a summary of the Château Pichon-Lalande archives and data contained in this work, which deals with Rauzan-Ségla.

The merchant of Bordeaux

Pierre Rauzan himself was not noble. Indeed, there is no evidence that his bourgeois origins stretch very far back. It is possible he was the grandson of a wealthy farmer and the son of a merchant, which would explain the bourgeois status he acquired around age 20. In an extremely hierarchical society, he compensated for this social handicap with other qualities. He was highly intelligent, a tireless worker, and – it would seem – very healthy, as he lived past 70 (he died in 1692). He was also ambitious, and eager to amass both fortune and repute. His 11 children lived to adulthood, which is quite exceptional at a time when, on average, one child in eight or ten survived past childhood. He seems to have lived his life under a lucky star, as he succeeded in almost everything he did. Undoubtedly, he was the kind of person who plays an influential role in the lives of those around him – a true force of nature.

A few major decisions, either good or bad, can determine the course of an entire life. Pierre Rauzan was no exception to this rule. He received the *bourgeois de Bordeaux* title in 1641, at a young age, acquiring certain privileges – vestiges of a time when Bordeaux was still ruled from London. The city's merchants enjoyed significant privileges in the English market: they paid no customs fees, and for many years had priority over the Haut Pays (the "upcountry" of Toulouse, Bergerac, and Gaillac) for selling their wines. At a time when next to nothing was known about preserving wines, selling one's products before Christmas was a significant advantage, as one could be sure that a wine made the same year would not spoil in the cold. The Haut Pays could only sell its wines after Christmas, and was thus subject to all the risks that came with the inexorable alteration of barreled wine, which was as yet un-sulfured. *Bourgeois de Bordeaux* were also allowed to bring the wine produced on their land into the city without paying taxes, even if that land lay outside the *bordelais* territory. Finally, the French monarchy, after it reclaimed the city from England, imposed lower taxes on them. It is clear, then, that the bourgeois title was much more than an honorific: it granted Pierre Rauzan access to a guild of powerful merchants who treasured their privileges and did everything they could to maintain them.

Until the Fronde, which broke out in Bordeaux in 1648, Rauzan's professional life taught him the skills of a great merchant, and his work brought him into contact with far-off lands. He traded in cured cod and wines, with no special regard to quality. The cod, known as *moulue*, or *morue verte*, was cured in brine or salted, but not dried. Its price placed it beyond the means of poorer customers. But cod fishing, along with the other great fishing trades, were slowly disappearing from Bordeaux, and Rauzan,

Right: the turmoil of *La Fronde*, a revolt not so much against a system – nascent absolutism – but against a man, Mazarin. This would prove to be its weakness. In the distance, one sees the Louvre and Notre-Dame de Paris. Engraving, 1650. Paris, Bibliothèque Nationale.

with his knack for adapting quickly to new situations, soon abandoned fishing and turned exclusively to wine.

The Fronde

In the 1640s, a political crisis known as the Fronde occurred. A rapid overview of this historical backdrop will be useful in understanding the choices made by Rauzan and Bernard de Pichon.

The Fronde, like all major crises in modern France, was a rebellion set off by taxes. But, unlike the 1789 Revolution, there were no *philosophes*, no ideologues, no politicians able to give it any social bent. Though the movement shook mid-17th century France with resurging waves of violence, it remained chaotic and disorganized, ultimately dying out and leaving the monarchy victorious.

Much was at stake in the conflict. Under Louis XIII and Richelieu, and then under the regency of Anne of Austria and Mazarin after 1643, France's leadership shifted from a monarchy with fairly lax governmental structures, most of them left over from another era, to a centralized modern state whose administration was increasingly demanding. At the time, the French crown was involved

AVIS QUE DONNE UN FRONDEUR AUX PARISIENS QU'IL EXORTE DE SE RÉVOLTER CONTRE LA TYRANNIE DU CARDINAL MAZARIN .

in a number of wars and required a considerable amount of money. Taxes rose precipitously. The only viable alternative would have been a decentralized federalist structure, with a central power tasked with specific responsibilities and some degree of autonomy left to the provinces. But the rebels, great nobles blinded by their hatred for Mazarin, were too undisciplined to rise above their immediate passions; they presented a weak and incoherent opposition to the political determination of Richelieu and then of Mazarin.

A few important figures are worthy of note at this juncture. In 1648, the *taille*, the main tax levied on the Bordeaux administrative district, jumped to more than

three million livres per year, compared to 1,300,000 livres in 1635. The *convoi et comptablie*, another tax, tripled between 1630 and 1634, and then rose another 75% by 1648. In 1635, heavy tariffs on barrels of wine sold at retail prices in taverns were introduced. That same year, when France went to war with Spain, it needed to fund the four armies it had deployed to its borders because the country was surrounded by Spanish possessions. Before 1630, the monarchy had spent some 40 million livres each year. The year war was declared, state spending soared to 200 million livres, leveling off at around 90 million. France's wealth, however, had not increased proportionately. Though other factors certainly came into play, the origins of the Fronde lie in these fiscal issues.

To detail all of the dramatic ins and outs of this crisis would lead us too far from our own path, so let us simply note that any Frenchman of some standing was rapidly confronted with the crucial question of which side to choose. That of the boy king, whose mother, Anne of Austria, and his minister, Mazarin, ruled in his stead? Or that of the rebels?

Deeming that wine taxation had soared to excessive heights, Bordeaux came out against the monarchy – against Paris, as usual. Both wine exports and wine served in taverns were heavily affected; even the *petit barricous* (little barrels) that Bordeaux residents brought home from visits to family or friends in the country were taxed upon entering the city. It is easy to understand their resentment toward the monarchy, whose armies besieged Bordeaux in 1650. The people of Bordeaux meant business: they were known to harass, mutilate, and even kill agents of the king.

Courtier royal

Popular sentiment, then, was far from peaceful. And yet, in the midst of all this tension, in July 1650, Pierre Rauzan purchased the title of *courtier royal* – royal wine broker – for 4,000 livres.* The objects of much disdain, these brokers were accused of "ensuring that all trade passed

BORDEAVX.

Above: 1661 engraving by Merian. By 1640, the port was exporting 540,000 hectolitres (14,300 gal) of wine, further whetting the tax collectors' appetites.
Left: Cardinal Jules Mazarin, aged 48 years, c. 1650. Though despised, Mazarin was exceptionally intelligent. He died in 1661, leaving a fortune of
35 million *livres*, including eight million in cash. Oil on canvas. Versailles, Château de Versailles and the Trianon.

through their hands" in a document dated 1652. Rauzan's decision to take on this role and to keep a level head while the Fronde raged around him, just a month before the King's troops launched their bloody siege, illustrates his strong will and physical courage; indeed, there could not have been much competition for such a position at that time. Peace was declared between Bordeaux and the king in September of the same year. True to form, the people of Bordeaux managed to devise a solution, promptly signing peace treaties as harvest season drew near: their livelihoods in the year to come depended on it.

Was Pierre Rauzan foolish or clever? We shall choose the latter hypothesis, which the next stage of his career confirms. Contemporary letters show that he kept a close eye on political and military events of the day, adapting

his business accordingly. A remarkable tactician, he crafted his strategy slowly and meticulously. It is very likely that he had carefully analyzed every aspect of the situation: high stakes call for precise calculation.

When the Fronde died out on its own, with a certain amount of upheaval along the way, Pierre Rauzan's choice to side with the monarchy – contrary to the major-

* In Bordeaux, *courtiers* purchased wines from producers and sold them to wine merchants, taking a commission for themselves in the process. A *courtier royal* did the same, but was also charged with collecting royal taxes and duties levied on wines. He purchased his position from the king, paying it off over a number of years. Though his position was an unpopular one, it nevertheless conferred a certain number of advantages: above all, the *courtier royal* was an agent of the king, and as such, all of his activities were protected by the crown.

Winemaker offering merchants a tasting and grape harvesters in the vines. The vines are planted in grove-like arbors rather than in trellised rows, a revolutionary technique which would reach the Médoc several decades later. Rows, which are much more practical, allow for plowing.
Oil on canvas, Flemish school, 1650. London, Sotheby's.

ity of his compatriots – proved to be quite advantageous. His rise had begun, and it would continue.

A great merchant

In 1652, Rauzan embarked on a partnership with Jean Thouvenin, and their trading company thrived, doing brisk business in wine and cod. Thouvenin sought out customers as far away as Brittany, while Rauzan supervised shipping and administration in Bordeaux. Their correspondence provides insight into that period.

The company enjoyed mounting success in the cod trade, but then turned exclusively to wine. In 1652, Rauzan shipped no less than 690 casks of wine – the equivalent of 2,760 Bordeaux export style barrels – to Amsterdam in several ships. Such figures bear witness to the considerable prominence he had attained by the end of the Fronde. The business was not without risk. Ships sailing to Brittany and Holland with cargo for distribution in northern Europe could sink or fall prey to pirates, but, as he notes, Rauzan insured his expeditions for "10,000 livres at 20%," and must have made a considerable amount of money. Two years later, he negotiated with 24 owners of what is now known as the Côtes de Bourg appellation, clinching a deal for 3,000 hectoliters (79,250 gallons), or 1,330 barrels, of wine.

Rauzan honed his judgment as he worked, gaining an ever-greater knowledge of the products he bought and sold in such terrific volume.

In a letter written on Christmas in 1653, he responds to Thouvenin, who has accused him of sending bad merchandise: "I am extremely surprised by such a rapid change, as I assure you that said wines were tasted, one by one, with great satisfaction." He continues, "You know that the wines I sent are the following *crus*: from Monsieur Dudon, 14 casks of wine, which is near Haut-Brion..." He then details the other wines in the shipment, concluding, "Of all these wines, I assure you that we have not one single cask that costs over 58 livres or more in the said region of Médoc."

This is an important letter. In it, Médoc wines make their first appearance in history. From there, they gained ground rapidly. It is worth noting that Rauzan praises Monsieur Dudon's wine, from "near the Haut-Brion." He already believes, in other words, that a wine from a location near a great *terroir* with a growing reputation, such as Haut-Brion, must be good. He would continue to promote this idea his whole life. But as we know from the days of the Fronde, Rauzan, a dyed-in-the-wool pioneer, was always a step ahead of his contemporaries.

By 1654, at the age of 35, Pierre Rauzan had separated from his associate and become a wealthy man. That year, he married Jeanne de Moncourier, who bore him 11 children and survived him by eight years. It would appear that he married for love. At his death, Pierre Rauzan left all powers to his wife even though his sons were nearly 40, asking that she divide things among their children as she saw fit. The scenario caused conflict between mother and sons at the execution of the will. This level of trust from a man used to calculating risk in his business dealings leads one to believe that Jeanne de Moncourier was well-loved. A career like Rauzan's, with its staggering series of successes, is difficult to imagine without constant emotional support to help him excel.

The master stroke: Château Margaux

Then came a major turning point in Rauzan's life; the moment, one might say, that he came into his own. On May 11, 1658, four years into his marriage and after the birth of his first four children, he signed a three-year lease for the Château Margaux and its outlying buildings, agreeing to pay 6,000 livres a year. In exchange, the owner of the Margaux barony, Jean Denis de Lestonnac d'Aulède, delegated all powers to Pierre Rauzan, along with the right to live in the château with his family.

What could have inspired our merchant to embark on this adventure? It is possible, though not certain, that it was the wine. That year, a 900-liter (240-gallon) cask of Château de Margaux sold for 78 livres, three livres less than certain Côtes de Bourg wines had four years before. Did Rauzan sense a changing tide for Margaux's wines? We know he had already been shipping Médoc wines for five years, and therefore was familiar with these wines and the prices they fetched from customers. He had tasted them, as he wrote in his letters, at least enough to speak about them with his business associate and defend the quality of his shipments. Could he have received some kind of decisive information from a local winemaker or an acquaintance from the Bordeaux market? There is no way of knowing. But what is certain is that a man like Rauzan would only have agreed to pay 6,000 livres a year if he expected to "come out on top," as he wrote.

In any case, Rauzan became a baron by proxy overnight, the lord of the land: he received not only revenues from the farmland, but also all feudal rents and dues the domain's peasants owed their lord. In some respects, these peasants were unrecognized landowners – they were said to "hold" (*tenir*) the lord's land, which was passed down from father to son, and as *tenanciers* (tenants) they were obliged to pay feudal dues to the lord, in money or in kind. If they decided to sell their *tenure* – or land holding, a form of property that strikes us as odd in this day and age – they were required to pay transaction fees known as *lods et ventes*. These fees varied, but if they went unpaid, the tenant had to sell and leave, or "decamp." Thanks to his new standing, Pierre Rauzan was in a real position of strength, with access to vital information on the financial situation of all the tenants living and working on the estate he oversaw. The contract provided him with a list, which he was required to return at the end of his lease, detailing each tenant and the dues they owed.

A control tower for the Médoc

In spite of this new status, our hero continued as a merchant and broker trading in wines, including wine from his new estate at Margaux. Pierre Rauzan now held sway over his profession, controlling the chain of production from top to bottom, from the peasant working the land to the local marketplace and its prices in Bordeaux to the customer in Amsterdam or London. One might call him the Médoc's control tower – and he continued to bolster his position as such. He was able to keep abreast of everything, as everything was – or would be – conducted through him.

Acting on the observation he made in the letter quoted above, Rauzan began purchasing land around the Château Margaux. He was well aware of the difficulties encountered by peasants under the feudal system and intimately acquainted with the feudal dues they owed the lord for whom he was acting as agent. He thus established what would become the Rauzan vineyards (Ségla and Gassie), under the Margaux appellation. His purchasing campaign was intense, and with the means available to him, he was able to build a fine estate very rapidly. At the same time, he became interested in other future

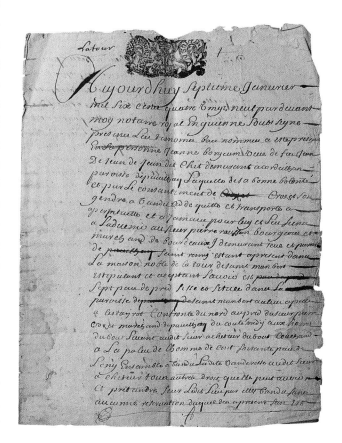

Médoc vineyards, stretching all the way to Saint-Estèphe, which he would manage. His position allowed him to systematically seek out unused land. He had, in fact, already grasped the implications of rising prices for Médoc wines in northern Europe: the Médoc was an area on the rise, to be invested in as quickly as possible. In fact, the Lord of Margaux took legal action against Rauzan, presumably because revenues from tenant farming seemed too low in relation to the staggering prices at which Rauzan, this peculiar farmer/merchant/broker, was selling his wines abroad. Indeed, something had changed in these "new" wines, inspired by Haut-Brion, which discerning London tasters like Samuel Pepys began to notice in 1663. They had a unique, even extraordinary taste – after people tasted them, they couldn't help but come back for more.

After Margaux, Latour

Pierre Rauzan was one of the first to notice this phenomenon, and what followed confirmed it. When his lease with Margaux ended, he signed another in 1679, at the age of 60, this time with Latour, in Pauillac. There, as he had at Margaux, he became lord by proxy. A cask of Latour cost 60 livres in 1679, and was sold at 200. This was already a good deal for Rauzan, but he must have known that the market was growing and that he could get even more for it. In 1678, the Treaty of Nijmegen brought the war with Holland to an end, and business was picking up again. At Latour, Rauzan faced a new kind of *terroir* and a new estate, with a new atmosphere that differed from Margaux – not to mention dozens of new tenants, whom he would get to know very quickly. Rauzan remained at Latour for 14 years until his death in 1692. The lease price is telling: he paid 5,320 livres yearly. The rent increased every time he renewed the agreement, reaching 6,600 livres in 1683 and 8,500 livres per year under a six-year contract in 1687 – an astronomical figure when one considers that a day's wages for a winemaker were eight to ten sous, or less than half

Contract for Pierre Rauzan of Latour's land purchase from Jeanne Bourgeum of Cordeillan. Deed dated January 7, 1689.

a livre. The figure reveals a new reality: wine prices had whetted the appetites of people like Rauzan, who understood their upward trend. In all, he paid more than 122,000 livres to run Latour over 13 years. According to historians, this would come to at least a million euros in today's currency. Latour, in other words, was a lucrative affair. Rauzan would never have agreed to pay so much money to its owners had he not believed he could make a great deal more from it.

Sulfur wick. The sulfur is lit and the hook is placed for several minutes in the bung (stopper) of the hermetically sealed oak barrel. Sulfur emissions sterilize the barrel.

Amassing land for the future Pichon-Longueville

As he had at Margaux, Rauzan rapidly began buying up the land around Latour, piecing together a new, modern wine estate, which would for many years be known as L'Enclos Rauzan and would constitute the core of Pichon-Longueville. This buying campaign continued at a frenzied pace, and peaked in 1686 to 1688, shortly before Rauzan's death. According to its official documents, the estate was equipped with carts and oxen, which would indicate that the vines were trellised in long rows rather than grown on arbors, as they still are in the Greek Isles. This more logical and profitable method contributed to the wine-growing revolution that the Médoc experienced in the Louis XIV era. L'Enclos Rauzan stretched to 21 hectares

(52 acres), of which 13 (32 acres) were planted with vines – a strong beginning. Its growth following Pierre Rauzan's death would slow considerably, since none of his successors had the same financial resources.

The birth of modern wines, preservation, and aging

As for the Médoc's wines during the Latour lease, a brief overview will clarify Pierre Rauzan's role in the revolution that would produce what the English called "new French clarets."

The rapid upswing in Médoc wine prices, in particular those of Margaux and Latour, as well as the financial litigations triggered by this change, indicate that something had happened to the very nature of the wines. Suddenly, their new taste made them more sought-after than other wines. The English name for them, "claret," tells us that they were light in color, and we know that the fermenting time following the harvest – at least up until the French Revolution – was short. But the flavor of these extraordinary *terroirs* had already begun to speak for itself. And thus questions surrounding their preservation and aging capacities, which would determine their prices, became central. Preserving and aging, which produced modern wines, was only possible by burning a bit of sulfur (a Dutch match or a sulfured wick) in the empty cask before filling it, thereby sterilizing it. But when was this preservation process first discovered? Examining Pierre Rauzan's documents may shed some light on this question.

The first written mention of the sulfured wick appears in 1729, in documents belonging to Rauzan's heirs, but nothing in them implies that the method is revolutionary or out of the ordinary. The practice, then, must have already existed – but since when?

In a letter dated May 6, 1684, sent from Bordeaux to Gilbon, his contact in Amsterdam, Pierre Rauzan provides an interesting piece of information. Gilbon had complained that the last shipment of wines tasted altered to him. "Not very natural," concedes Rauzan, con-

A barrel with the Pichon-Longueville Comtesse de Lalande seal (the initials PLL topped by the crown of a marquis, the Lalande title).

tinuing, "This means you will be obliged to sell, instead of cellaring it. I will be pleased with what you do, believing as I do that you will act appropriately. I nevertheless believe that, while they are not entirely perfect, *something still remains of their good quality* [italics added for emphasis] and that there are very few wines of this sort. Do therefore as you see fit. I will be entirely satisfied."

This letter shows that, in 1684, methods for preserving wine in warm temperatures beyond an entire year, or even less, were still unknown. For if the sulfur wick had existed, a merchant as powerful as Pierre Rauzan would have used it, if only because it was in his immediate financial interest. We may say with near certainty, then, that the method did not yet exist, and that the new wines consumed in London were produced within the last year at the very most.

But the story changes in 1695, evidenced by a court case brought by Rauzan's sons against their mother, Jeanne de Moncourier, following their father's death. Among other things, they accuse her of not including in the inheritance the casks of wine in their cellar from 1690 and the following years, "great wines and secondary wines," the former valued "at the highest prices among all wines." Their contest of the will revolved around the considerable volume of 462 casks containing 900 liters (240 gallons) of vintage, some dating back five years.

Rauzan's sons would never have fought their mother so vigorously over these older wines if they had known they would turn after a year in a barrel and were good for nothing more than to be thrown into the Garonne river. We may thus assume that by 1690, the past six years had taught Rauzan how to preserve wines. At the very latest, the sulfured wick may have appeared in time to preserve the 1690 vintage; otherwise, a fierce legal battle between Rauzan's sons and their mother would have been absurd. Their arguments, in legalistic language impossible

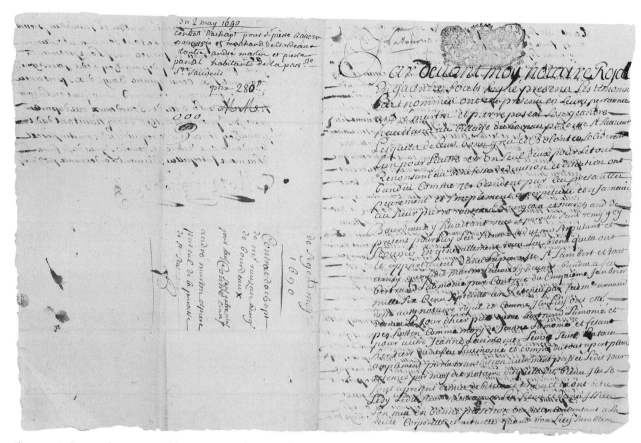

Above: a 280-*livre* purchase contract *"du sieur Rauzan, bourgeois de Bordeaux,"* for a property of André Martin and Pierre Pascal, from the parish of Saint-Sauveur near Pauillac.

Right: engraved portrait of Bernard de Pichon as second President of the Bordeaux Parliament, c. 1650.

to reproduce here, show they were fully attuned to the preservation issue.

We find another hint in Château Haut-Brion's history. Documents indicate that the 1695 vintage could be kept for over three years. René Pijassou notes that in such cases it was sold at 150 livres a cask*. The two dates' proximity is interesting: yet again, we see Rauzan was ahead of his time, as his sons believed a 1690 vintage was still sellable in 1695. Furthermore, the Château Haut-Brion, like other châteaux, stopped exporting when the War of the League of Augsburg broke out in autumn 1688, pitting France against a large coalition that included Holland and England, both great maritime powers and importers of Bordeaux wines. England restricted wine imports, leaving producers and merchants with extensive unsold stock, a possible explanation for Pierre

Rauzan's reserves. Preservation would thus have been an urgent problem: losing such costly wines was unthinkable. Perhaps they applied the new technique – perhaps tested elsewhere – of burning sulfur in empty casks.

With luck, other documents will further clarify this question; for now, it seems impractical to draw any conclusions beyond these hints, which would locate the art of aging and preserving wines around 1690.

A trailblazer

Pierre Rauzan died in 1692, leaving everything to his wife. His youngest daughter, Thérèse, born in 1672, married

* R. Pijassou, *Le Médoc, un grand vignoble de qualité*, Paris, Tallandier, 1980, p. 349.

Jacques-François de Pichon in 1694, and was given L'Enclos Rauzan as a dowry. Thérèse Rauzan, the future baroness of Pichon-Longueville, thus brought Pierre Rauzan's work to fruition in the form of the Pichon-Longueville vineyard. Much remained to be done to create a prestigious winegrowing estate, but this was for the following century.

Pierre Rauzan was a truly unusual character. From his beginnings in cured cod and coarse *vins de palus* from the Gironde, he kept up with Bordeaux's winegrowing revolution, and indeed was part of its vanguard. The Médoc owes him much. He would not live to see the immense success of the great Médoc wines in the following century, nor to see his daughter Thérèse become a baroness and take the helm of a renowned vineyard. As is true of all pioneers, his greatest accomplishment was passing on his legacy. Surprisingly, for nearly a century it was women who followed in Rauzan's footsteps and consolidated his accomplishments.

BERNARD DE PICHON

Bernard de Pichon (1610-1684) had been dead for ten years when his youngest son married Pierre Rauzan's daughter. Though he had no role in the vineyard, he garnered royal favor during the Fronde, bringing social prominence to his family. He created a legacy that would continue for two centuries, establishing the Pichon-Longuevilles as loyal servants of the Bourbons.

A parliament member from Bordeaux

Notwithstanding the dubious genealogies some noble families had made in the 19th century, when they had lost everything but their names, we see that the Pichons were recent nobility under Louis XIII.

There are both noble and non-noble Pichon families in France, with different geographical origins, in Brittany, Languedoc, and Guyenne. Bernard de Pichon's family hailed from the latter, and research reveals with near certainty that they were ennobled in 1577 by letters patent. François de Pichon was the first Pichon to make a career in the Parlement de Bordeaux, and eventually became its second president, marrying Catherine de Bavolier, the daughter of another président, in 1602. They gave birth to Bernard around 1610.

Bernard enjoyed a brilliant career, and was named second président of the Parlement de Bordeaux, too. His first wife died, leaving him with a daughter, Finette de Pichon. He then married Anne d'Affis, a widow and member of the old *noblesse d'épée*, or "nobility of the sword," who gave him the château and barony of Longueville as well as two sons. Strategic marriages were common throughout the Pichon family's history.

Before we continue, however, it is important to understand fully the *parlements* of Ancien Régime France, particularly since the Parlement de Bordeaux played a significant role for the Médoc's *grands crus*.

The *parlements* of the Ancien Régime

Under the Ancien Régime, a *parlement* (or parliament) differed greatly from what we understand by this word today. At that time, a French *parlement* was an assembly of unelected dignitaries who had purchased their positions, acquiring membership in the *noblesse de robe* ("nobility of the cloth"). They could then transmit their titles to their descendants for a lower price. The assembly's functions varied. It acted as a court of justice, in that cases could be appealed before it as a last resort. As such, it was a sovereign institution, and acted as a sort of guardian of the kingdom's fundamental laws, a kind of "unwritten, common-law constitution," according to Michel Pernot. None of the king's edicts, laws, or ordinances could go into effect before being registered with the *parlement* in the region where they were to be applied. The *parlement* could make "humble remonstrances," or respectful objections, if they considered that the proposed legislation did not comply with the kingdom's laws. The king, following a special formal procedure called the *lit de justice*, had the final say, but the *parlement* managed to carry out some legislative work: specific provisions were occasionally modified.

Because they were unable to transform themselves into an autonomous political power, *parlements* were ultimately eliminated during the French Revolution. While critical of the political system, they depended on it entirely, and were therefore never able to rally as a genuine agent of reform, with the power to help the government evolve from an absolute monarchy to a limited or constitutional one. On the other hand, it is unclear whether this could have been possible, given that their members were unelected and had purchased their positions. This conundrum, in which they risked losing everything if they lost the king, is a little-understood fact in the history of France. The *parlements* were what Emmanuel Leroy Ladurie tidily referred to as *fossoyeurs inhumés*, or buried gravediggers.

In Bordeaux, these dignitaries often owned major vineyards producing *grands crus*, and played a key role in the constant pursuit of quality in their wines.

A leader of the Fronde in Bordeaux

Parlement members were thus at the forefront of the rebellion against the king in the 17th century, and went so far as to eliminate certain taxes enacted by royal power in 1648, gaining considerable popularity. After the *premier président* appointed by the king fled, Bernard de Pichon often served as a political leader and was known as the *grand président* despite his second-rank position. His popularity continued to rise, peaking in October 1649.

The Duc d'Épernon, a royal representative who led a force of 10,000 well-trained men who were bitterly detested by the people of Bordeaux, controlled the Château Trompette at the mouth of the port. He built a citadel at Libourne to cut off and starve out Bordeaux by forbidding its provisioning by sea or by the Dordogne river.

The city snapped into action, organizing a small, improvised army to attack the fortifications while they were still under construction. The conflict ended in a bloody stalemate. The elderly Marquis de Chambaret, Bordeaux's military chief, was killed, along with many others. D'Épernon's troops went on a destructive rampage, raping, pillaging, burning vineyards, and razing fruit trees to the ground. Once unleashed, the fury of the battle did not abate. To avoid total calamity, a peace treaty between Mazarin and Bordeaux was signed on Christmas 1649. Amnesties were granted, taxes lowered, and the Libourne fortress was demolished.

But the Fronde returned in even greater force when one of its members, the Grand Condé, a prince who had defeated the Spanish in battle, was arrested in January

Arrival of Louis XIV in Bordeaux. The young king (age 13) is welcomed by the municipal magistrates. Behind these two, on the left, we see Bernard de Pichon with his long hair and generous beard. Standing behind Louis XIV is the queen mother and regent, Anne of Austria. Engraving, 1650. Paris, Bibliothèque Nationale.

1650. His sister sought asylum in Bordeaux. That spring was an eventful one: bloody fighting broke out again, and the rebellion continued, sometimes amid near-comical episodes. Bernard de Pichon, who was in charge of the artillery during an engagement, managed to escape harm, with only his horse shot out from under him. That summer, the Duc d'Épernon retaliated against Bernard by burning down his Lormont château, which stood opposite Bordeaux on the other side of the Garonne river. In their furor toward Mazarin, the great lords went so far as to stir up popular revolt. New and much more radical demands were made, including some that foreshadowed those of the French Revolution in the following century. Bernard de Pichon had already lost his ancestral château, and was no longer willing to support a movement whose increasingly revolutionary bent seemed dangerous to him. He chose to side with the king, inspiring the hatred of many people, yet refusing to turn back, even when slandered and physically threatened.

New negotiations began, and Mazarin persuaded the young Louis XIV to come to Bourg, not far from the rebellious city, with his mother, Anne of Austria. Bernard de Pichon was chosen to address the king in August 1650 to request clemency for his compatriots, who had named him their political leader. In an extremely eloquent speech, he reminded Louis XIV that, to rule as a king, that he must first win the hearts of his subjects. The king never forgot this advice.

The situation abated and seemed to be over; the 1650 grape harvest was carried out as usual. The Duc d'Épernon was driven away, and the Grand Condé arrived in the city triumphantly the following year. But popular sentiment had been awakened, and the people's demands would give rise to a new Fronde, known as the Ormée. The movement, linked to the English Revolution, was more radical, foreshadowing certain aspects of Jacobinism. It swept Bordeaux and terrorized the city, lashing out at Bernard de Pichon, who had become the insurgents' whipping boy. By then, they had organized themselves into a sort of local *commune*. In an operation that pushed the movement toward civil war, they mobilized 2,000 men and attacked his home with cannons in

July 1653. Bernard de Pichon and his men fired from the windows in self defense. It took the Church's intervention to prevent the crowd from burning down the building, or what was left of it. Bernard de Pichon and his family took refuge in a friend's château. Twice now, his political positions – first against and then in favor of the king – had cost him everything he owned.

His career is an excellent illustration of the ambiguous standing of the *parlements*, which were never able to take their criticism of the monarchy beyond a certain point.

The king's favor

The Ormée uprising was quelled, peace returned, and King Louis XIV gave his loyal servant sufficient recompense for his difficulties. Later, when the king went to meet his future wife, Maria Theresa of Spain, he stopped at Bernard de Pichon's home on the way there, and then on the way back with the new queen of France. Anne of Austria made him the executor for certain charitable works she had named in her will.

From that time onward, Bernard de Pichon's descendants received the constant support of France's kings, offering them unwavering loyalty in return.

The Pichon-Longueville line

Bernard's oldest son inherited his fortune and repurchased his father's *parlement* position. He founded the Pichon-Parempuyre branch of the family. Bernard's second son, Jacques-François, was left with nothing and became a soldier. In 1694, the king's intendant gave him permission to take the name and title of his mother, Anne d'Affis de Longueville. He married Thérèse de Rauzan and became the first baron of Pichon-Longueville.

Like the confluence of two great rivers, their marriage brought together two of Bordeaux's most prominent families. From their union flows the Pichon-Longueville *cru.*

LADIES OF THE VINE

Surprising as it may seem, the Pichon-Longueville vineyard was overseen by women for the greater part of the 18th century. As elsewhere, a *régisseur* – an estate steward, or overseer – ensured the continuity of onsite management. But, at least between 1717 and 1780, ultimate responsibility, as well as new land purchases and major decisions, lay mostly in the hands of three women: Thérèse de Rauzan, Germaine de Lajus, and Marie Branda de Terrefort. Each was married to a Pichon-Longueville heir and took responsibility of the estate for considerable periods once their husbands reached old age or died prematurely. And each of them did a fine job: right before the French Revolution, they had brought the vineyard to *troisième cru* status according to the price rankings of the time (it would be considered a *deuxième cru* by the 1820s). The great wine's feminine influence, so strong in the 18th and 19th centuries, continues today under May-Eliane de Lencquesaing, who ushered the Comtesse de Lalande into the 20th century. These 18th-century "ladies of the vine" should be remembered alongside the men known in the Médoc as "princes" or "lords" of the vine for generations.

Keeping time with the *livre de rentes*

The Château Latour's *livre de rentes*, the official record book of the estate's feudal rents, survives in the Pichon-Longueville Comtesse de Lalande archives. It is an exceptional document that, in conjunction with other data, provides us with vital information from the 18th century. Since the land Pierre Rauzan had purchased was part of the Château Latour's estate, he and his successors were required to pay significant feudal rents every year when the grape harvest came. Whatever the volume of the harvest, they paid their landlord a sum of money and a cask of wine, or four barrels (a significant amount since production sometimes fell as low as nine casks). Every year, the tenant paid his or her feudal rents on a given date, and it was recorded in the *livre de rentes*. Latour's estate steward then signed the notebook. The *livre de rentes* in the Pichon-Longueville Comtesse de Lalande archives documents payments between 1717 and 1780.

We know, therefore, whether Monsieur of Madame Pichon was present at each harvest to pay the feudal rents. We also know that the baron or baroness of

Pichon-Longueville lived either in Bordeaux or in the Château de Longueville near Marmande. The master of the estate always came to oversee the grape harvest, ensuring that it went smoothly and discussing important decisions for the year to come with the estate steward. In other words, the *livre de rentes* tells us who managed the vineyard along with the estate steward. When we compare this information with the various family members' birth and death dates, the data match up astoundingly well. Once we also take into account the written record of land purchases made by these women, the feminine side of history emerges quite distinctly from these documents, like a photograph coming into focus as it is developed.

Above: the Château Latour ledger certifying that "Madame de Rausan de Longueville," as the seigneur de Latour's vassal, had duly made her feudal payment in cash and in kind, October 31, 1724.

A unique engraving showing the facilities and houses on the Pichon-Longueville property before the construction of the two current châteaux. Purchased by Pierre Rauzan, the house was called *de Badern* ("old fogy's house"). The estate steward lived there during the year, and the master or mistress came for the harvest. Note also that the vines are planted in rows.

Thérèse de Rauzan

Up until 1777, Pichon-Longueville was ruled by three barons: Jacques-François (1649-1731), Jacques (1697-1752), and Jean-Pierre (1731-1761).

The first was Bernard de Pichon's youngest son, who at the age of 43 married 20-year-old Thérèse de Rauzan. As a younger son, he had no right to inherit, and set off on a military career. The many wars fought by Louis XIV must have given him ample occasion to distinguish himself in battle, but his rank is unknown. He undoubtedly served the King of Poland, Jean Sobieski, a defender of Christendom who defeated the Ottoman Turks at Kahlenberg and married a French woman, Marie d'Arquien. After his family had lost power, Sobieski's son came to present Jacques-François with a sword at the Château de Longueville, perhaps for some military feat or act of courage. Could it have been against the

Ottomans? This is possible, as Jacques-François's Christian faith ran deep. During his life, he made a trip to Rome to obtain indulgences for himself, his parents, and friends through fasting, prayers, and penitence.

Whatever his religious convictions, he must have been very different from his young wife, who grew up in the bourgeois milieu of the wine trade that we have already explored. While she was heir to a family tradition of wine-making and learned tangible skills during her childhood (aside from her sisters, who took the veil, all of the Rauzan children were involved in wine production), her husband must not have been particularly versed in a business that had not yet taken on the scope it would later have.

Though the baron paid the feudal rents in 1717 and 1718 (nothing is known before these dates), Thérèse, to whom documents sometimes refer as Baronne Rausan de Longueville, took over in 1719 and 1720, and then came to pay the feudal rents at every grape harvest from 1723 to 1746, the year of her death. Thérèse also took over and pursued Pierre Rauzan's land purchasing policy. Numerous land purchase contracts from well before 1717 bear her signature. Signed at Saint-Lambert or at Pauillac in January, February, March, or May, they attest to her strong presence in the Médoc. She closely monitored the vineyard she had inherited from her father; in time, she would pass it on to her own son, in good working order. The length of time necessary for a return on investment on vines planted for a *grand cru* was a very real concept for her: one always plants for the next generation.

At the same time, Thérèse's brothers were upgrading the Rauzan vineyard in Margaux in order to reach the highest level of quality. A number of business and legal dealings went on between her and her brothers, mainly regarding issues of inheritance. Occasionally, she won, though more often than not her cases were dismissed. This shows that she was well aware of the progress they had made, and that a silent rivalry among Pierre Rauzan's children was one of the factors that drove her. With a clear view of everything at stake, she threw herself into developing her dowry and her father's legacy.

By examining and comparing archival documents, we can safely determine that, until the mid-18th century, Pichon-Longueville was run by a woman – a woman who was also a Rauzan.

Germaine de Lajus

Jacques de Pichon-Longueville succeeded his mother for five short years, first coming to pay the feudal rents to the Lord of Latour in 1747. He was a member of the *parlement* and unquestionably preferred life in Bordeaux. It is possible that his health was delicate; in any case, he died in 1752. In 1751, he passed his political responsibilities to his oldest son, Jean-Pierre, who was just 19 and needed special

Opposite: a record of Pierre and Thérèse de Rauzan's papers, which was put together by Germaine de Lajus upon the death of her husband.
It is a lengthy but regrettably incomplete list of land sales and exchange contracts from the Pichon-Longueville property.

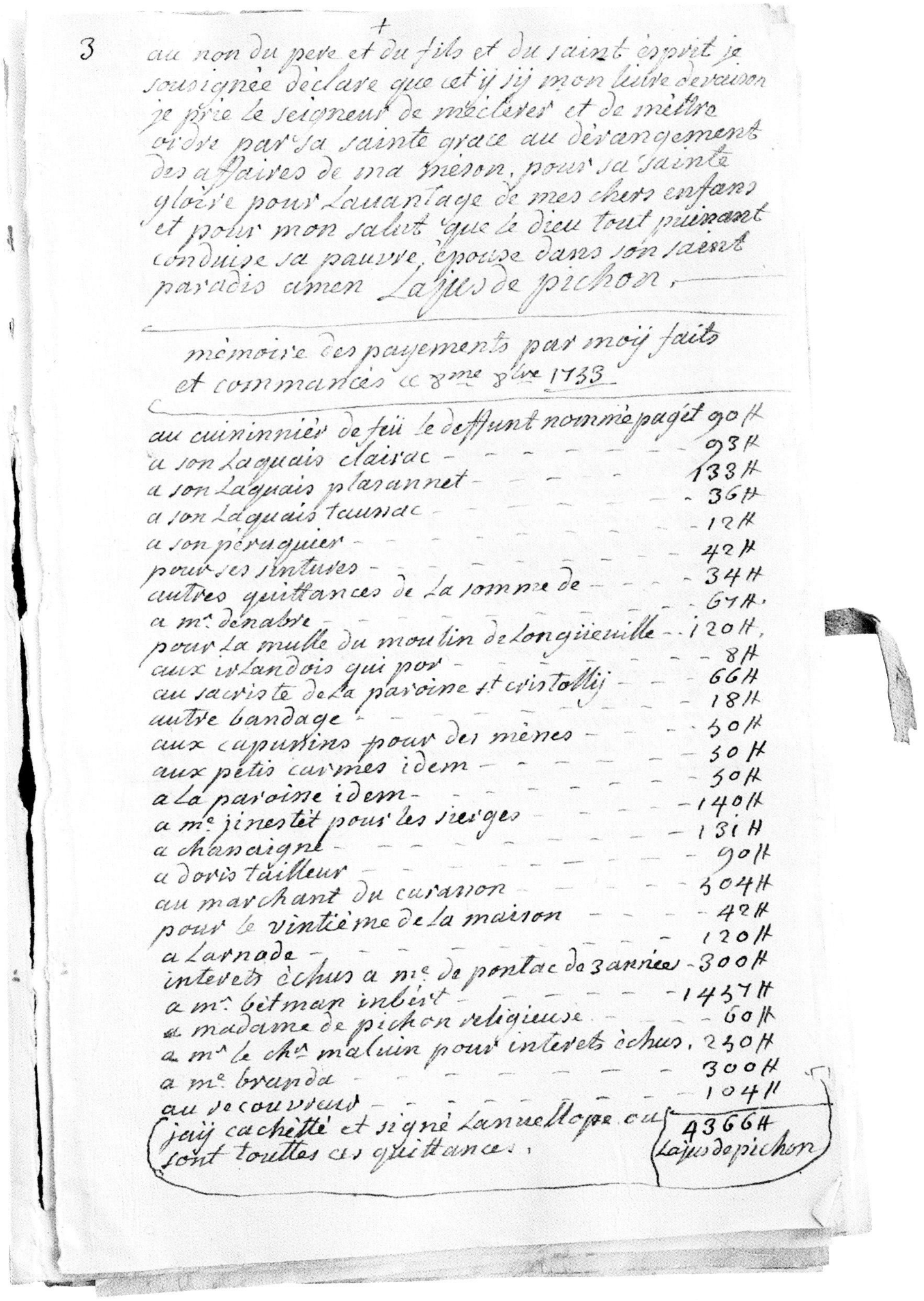

3

au non du pere et du fils et du saint esprit je
sousignée déclare que cy sy mon livre deraison
je prie le seigneur de m'éclerer et de mettre
ordre par sa sainte grace au dérangement
des affaires de ma meson, pour sa sainte
gloire pour l'auantage de mes chers enfans
et pour mon salut que le dieu tout puissant
conduise sa pauvre épouse dans son saint
paradis amen Lajus de pichon,

memoire des payements par moy faits
et commancés ce 8me 8bre 1733

au cuirinnier de feü le deffunt nommé pagét	90 H
a son laquais clairac	93 H
a son laquais plarannet	133 H
a son laquais taunac	36 H
a son péruquier	12 H
pour ses sintures	42 H
autres quittances de la somme de	34 H
a mr denabre	67 H
pour la mulle du moulin de longüeville	120 H
aux irlandois qui por	8 H
au sacriste de la paroine st cristollij	66 H
autre bandage	18 H
aux capurtins pour des mênes	50 H
aux pétis carmes idem	50 H
a la paroine idem	50 H
a mr jinestet pour les sierges	140 H
a chancaigne	131 H
a doris tailleur	90 H
au marchant du caranon	504 H
pour le vintième de la maison	42 H
a larnade	120 H
interets échus a mr de pontac de 3 annèes	300 H
a mr bétman inbert	1437 H
a madame de pichon religieuse	60 H
a mr le chr maluin pour interets échus	230 H
a mr branda	300 H
au secourceur	104 H

j'ay cachetté et signé Lannellope ou
sont toutes ces quittances.

4366 H
Lajus de pichon

The accounts ledger of Germaine de Lajus, signed "Lajus de Pichon," opened with a moving prayer. Accounts are drawn up in the *"livres tournois"* currency.

dispensation to hold a seat in the Parlement de Bordeaux – with no deliberative voting rights – before the legal age. Jacques must have already been ill and may have known that he was not long for this world. He passed away without leaving any major mark on this history.

His wife, Germaine de Lajus, took over the vineyards and had an inventory made of the official papers belonging to Pierre Rauzan and his daughter Thérèse, a document that is now at Pichon-Lalande. The Château Latour's *livre de rentes* shows that she came to pay the feudal rents from 1752 to 1758; she died the following year. The vineyard was extremely productive under her direction:

more than 60 casks of wine were made in 1754 and 1755 from less than 20 hectares (49 acres) of grapevines, quite a remarkable achievement at a time when average production rarely went above 15 hectoliters per hectare (162 gallons per acre).

We still have the personal account book that Germaine de Lajus kept for the entire time she ran Pichon. In it, we see that she monitored the Médoc estate's management very closely and rigorously. She kept track of yearly production, wine sales, vineyard upkeep, and domestic expenses, "praying," as she wrote, "that the Lord bring light and order through his Holy Grace to all that disrupts my household." Widowed at a young age, Madame de Lajus de Pichon wore plain black cotton dresses. Among other costs, she is recorded as having paid a merchant for vine stakes, which confirms information found in official documents: in 1752, the vineyard was indeed trellised, and had kept pace with the Médoc's winegrowing revolution.

Germaine de Lajus de Pichon was a kind woman who survived the death of her husband and her first two grandsons with undisputable grace. Following in the footsteps of her predecessor, Thérèse de Rauzan, she guided the vineyard with rigor and care.

Marie Branda de Terrefort

Like his male predecessors, Jean-Pierre, the third baron, died early. The *livre de rentes*, that faithful timekeeper, tells us that he came to pay the feudal rents for just two years. He died in 1761 at the age of 30, possibly of the same illness as his father, leaving behind a 25-year-old widow and two small children. They had married when he was 16, and she only 11, evidence of a great fear of illness (possibly

tuberculosis) and of the family line's disappearance. For the 17 years following his death, his widow, Marie Branda de Terrefort, presided over the vineyard. In addition to ordinary upkeep, she bought as much land as her means permitted, cleared fields (of which one still bears her name), and had them planted with vines. Her presence is noted at every year's grape harvests until her death in 1777, at 41.

The following year, her elder daughter and her younger son Joseph – the "Pichon heirs," as the *livre de rentes* calls them – came to pay the feudal dues for two years. The sister then disappears from record. Thus, at age 19, the young Baron Joseph de Pichon-Longueville began his long reign.

Pichon-Longueville before the French Revolution

Pierre Rauzan had been able to do very little for the vineyard he built shortly before his death. Three women were largely responsibly for Pichon-Longueville until 1777, and made it a *troisième cru*. René Pijassou established the *cru* classification system based on data from broker Abraham Lawton. Between 1760 and 1770, depending on the year, a cask of Pichon-Longueville sold for between 365 and 540 livres, the same price as estates like Ducru-Beaucaillou (then Bergeron), which, like Pichon, moved to the rank of *deuxième cru* the following century. *Premiers crus* like Latour and Lafite went for between 800 and 1,800 livres, while *deuxièmes crus* such as Mouton, Rauzan, and Léoville were priced between 600 and 800.

Nearly a century's work by these three ladies of the vine had brought forth praiseworthy results.

Baron Jean-Pierre de Pichon-Longueville, pastel
by Jean-Baptiste Perroneau (1715-1783), in 1756. Private collection.
Right page: The Wine Harvest, Francisco de Goya (1746-1828).
Revealing a lesser-known side of this painter, who died in Bordeaux,
these tapestry cartoons show an intensely poetic character, not unlike
that of the young Victor Hugo remembering his childhood in a Spain
ravaged by the Napoleonic Wars. Tapestry cartoon, 1786. Madrid,
Museo del Prado.

Baron Joseph (1760-1849)

Joseph de Pichon-Longueville was born in 1760, under Louis XV. He died at almost 90 in December 1849, during the second Republic, under the presidency of Louis Napoléon. Over his lifetime, he witnessed three revolutions, five kings, two republics, and an empire. He watched the era of the horse give way to steam transport. He fathered five children, surviving his brother Jean-Jacques, his sister Jeanne Germaine, and his own son, Louis. Several of his children died shortly after he did, having lived out the majority of their lives during his own. It was Joseph who brought Pichon-Longueville to the rank of *second cru*. The lives of Joseph and his children were so full of action, so peopled with strong personalities, so fraught with momentous philosophical and political questions, that their stories could easily be the inspiration for a great historical novel.

Total commitment

It would seem that the young Joseph had a fairly fragile constitution: it was decided that, instead of entering the Parlement de Bordeaux, he oversee the farming of his lands, without straining himself to excess. This was a lucky thing for Pichon-Longueville, because Joseph devoted all of his energy and intelligence to developing the vineyard. His marriage in 1784 to Marguerite de Narbonne-Pelet d'Anglade was yet another stroke of luck. Lest the reader be misled by her title, we should add that Marguerite's father, Jacques Pelet, built up an impressive fortune and acquired his nobility by chance, through a series of cleverly won lawsuits, substantial gifts, and a marriage to a distant cousin of the Baron Joseph. But his daughter boasted an irresistible dowry of 150,000 livres. Joseph promised a more modest dower* of 2,000 livres in rent and 10,000 livres for "more ample jewels," but he also brought with him both the barony and the vineyard. With such resources, Joseph was able to adopt the most modern farming methods of the time, and made extensive land purchases. His contracts numbered in the dozens, and at his death, the vineyard stretched over 50 hectares (124 acres). This had a very rapid effect on the vineyard's production, which, before the Revolution, reached a record 81 casks in 1786.

The young couple had a daughter, Sophie, in 1785; a boy, Raoul-Albert (whom we will call Raoul), in 1787; and a second son, Louis, in 1789.

* A dower consists of provisions for support accorded by a husband to his wife; in France at the time these generally consisted of the usufruct of properties for the surviving widow.

The beginning of the Revolution

When the Revolution broke out, we can be sure that – in the beginning, at least – Joseph, who was very much a man of the Enlightenment, was in favor of it. After all, it abolished the feudal rents he had to pay to Latour and to the Château Beychevelle for the land he owned within the Saint-Julien parish. We also have the last Beychevelle *livre de rentes*, which begins in 1788, when Joseph reportedly paid 350 livres for seven years of unpaid rents. The *livre de rentes* ends that same year: clearly, the rents went unpaid because of the Revolution. Unfortunately, the ledger preceding it has been lost. We know that many aristocrats applauded the advent of the Revolution, and indeed acted as political leaders in its first phase. Comte Fumel was mayor of Bordeaux, Jean-François de Boisancourt was the director of the Grand Théâtre, Maréchal de Duras commanded the *garde nationale*, etc.

All evidence leads us to believe that Joseph followed this trend. In any case, he did what the Revolution expected of him: he joined the *garde nationale*, paid his contribution, took out all the necessary memberships, and pronounced the required oaths. Finally, it is more than likely that he purchased Church properties. Everyone, even Marie-Antoinette did so. Their sales were intended to pay off the towering debt that the King had incurred in France's name. One thing is certain: following the Revolution, his wines were produced in great quantity, indicating that the estate had grown during this first phase of sales of national goods. Louis d'Estournel did the same to extend the bounds of Cos d'Estournel.

Flight to the Médoc

Retracing the course of the Revolution in Bordeaux – recreating its atmosphere, painting its varied personalities – would be too lengthy a task for this book. The Civil Constitution of the Clergy was a grave error on the part of the Constituent Assembly, both in that it touched the consciences and religious beliefs of the French people, and in that it had been instituted without consulting the Pope, which led to the king's flight and his arrest at Varennes in June 1791. The schism between the two halves of France grew wider, moving toward civil war, and political radicalization stretched far beyond Paris.

Then, the newly elected Legislative Assembly thrust the country into a war for which it was not prepared, bringing a series of disasters and endangering the *patrie*.*

By the end of spring 1792, a shrewder and more cautious Joseph left Bordeaux with his entire family. To escape the dangers of the city, he decided to move to Pichon, in the Médoc, into his house among the vineyards.

As soon as he arrived – we see his prudence and sensible attitude in his actions – he joined the Pauillac *garde nationale* and the local society of *sans-culottes*, which included several lords, opened accounts for the poor at the baker's and the butcher's, and took all of the required civic oaths. Things in the countryside were calmer, and support from his network of vine workers was significant. Joseph was thus able to avoid the fact that his younger brother, Jean-Jacques, had joined the émigré army abroad. At Pichon, he and his family enjoyed a peaceful year, hoping that the storm of the Revolution would pass.

At the same time, over the summer, the King was toppled by insurrection and the Republic proclaimed. The trial and execution of Louis XVI in January 1793 served to deepen the divide within the French people, and uprisings in the Vendée continued; meanwhile, the French army was having trouble holding fast to its positions abroad. The military *putch* staged in the Convention on May 5, 1793, followed by the arrest of the Girondin deputies and the assassination of Marat, created a climate of dramatic uncertainty throughout that fateful summer of 1793.

---

* *Patrie* has been variously translated as nation, homeland, fatherland, motherland, and country. In the case of the French Revolution, it meant all of these.

French Revolution. Issuance of a certificate of non-aristocratic origin under the Terror. Constant surveillance, fueled by frequent denunciations, made room for countless abuses and general corruption. Colored copper engraving, 1793.

Prisoners under the Terror

On September 5, the Terror was unleashed, and the alarming Law of Suspects was enacted. The law, according to which one could be arrested for simple "indifference" to the Revolution, heralded the totalitarian regimes of the modern era. By autumn, the Terror had caught up with Joseph: following a denunciation, he and his wife were arrested in October, accused of being *aristocrates renforcés* – entrenched aristocrats – by the revolutionary committee in Lesparre, Médoc. Under the Jacobins, denunciation was considered a public virtue.

In spite of harsh prison conditions in Lesparre, Joseph defended himself, mobilizing his networks and producing all of the necessary papers, certificates, and testimonies, insisting that he was a simple farmer who lived off the fruits of his labors and had never emigrated. He and his wife, Marguerite de Pelet d'Anglade, were released. But catastrophe struck when, following a denunciation, a warrant was issued for the arrest of his father-in-law, the fabulously wealthy Jacques de Pelet, whose sons had emigrated to fight the new Republic. Joseph and his wife were arrested again, while Jacques de Pelet d'Anglade fled and went into hiding. His home was searched. The search turned up nothing more than some satirical songs against the Revolution; this, however, was a grave offense, since

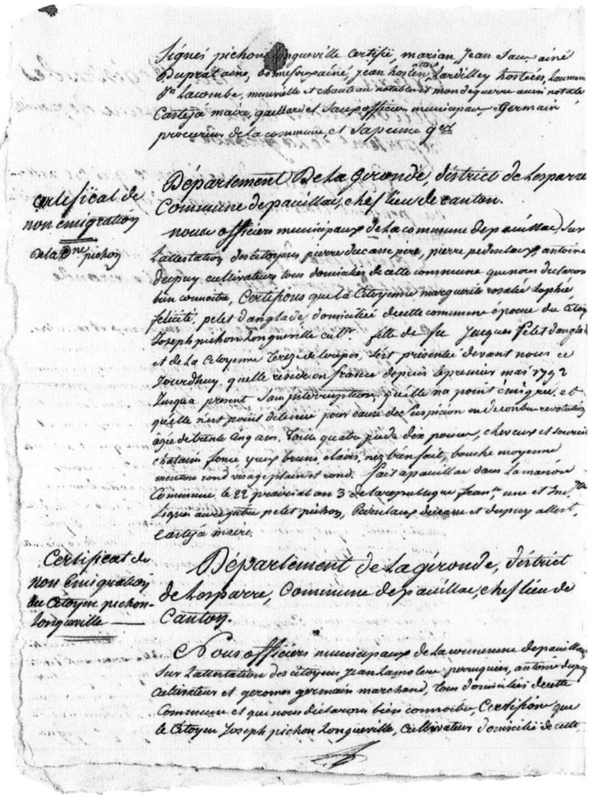

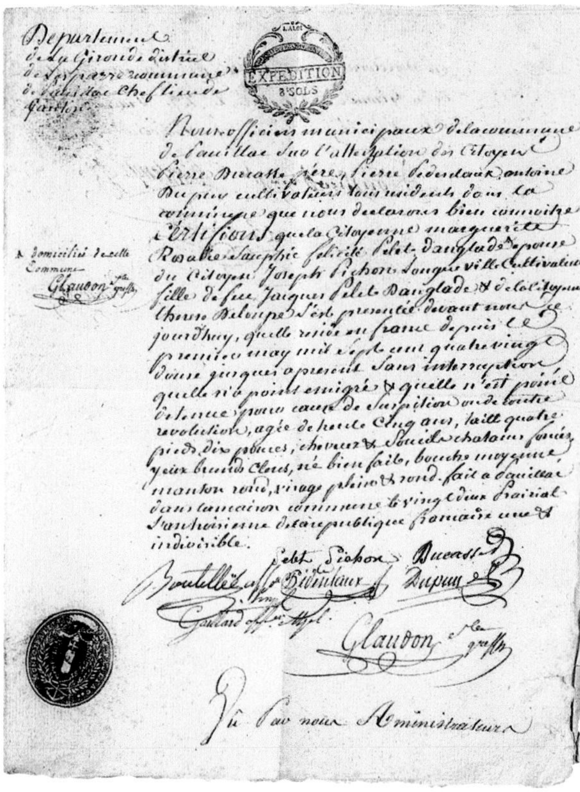

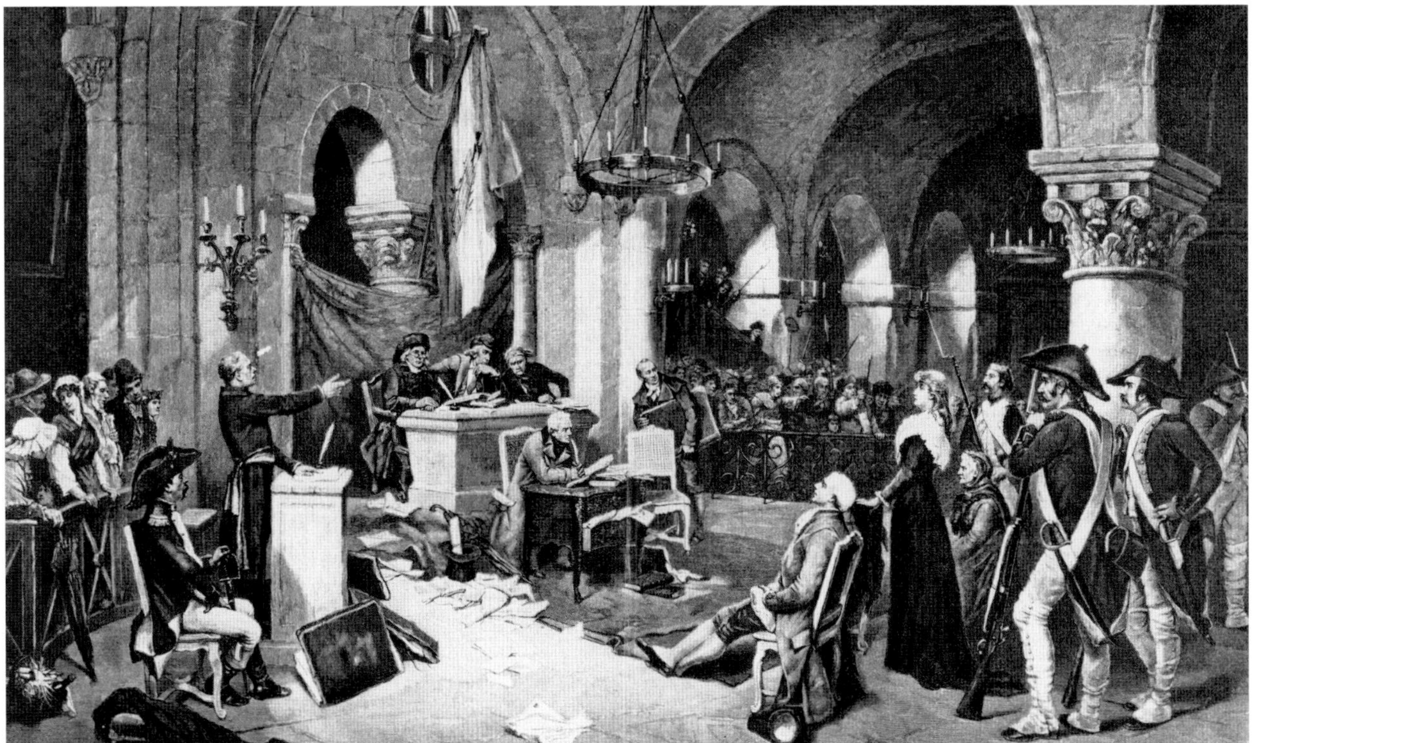

Upper left: *certificats de non-émigration* (documents stating that the bearer was not an émigré) of the citizeness Pichon-Longueville in 1794. These papers had to be renewed frequently. Note the word *certifions* ("we certify") written in bold, and her husband Joseph's profession: *cultivateur*.
Below: *Un tribunal sous la Terreur* (*A Tribunal under the Terror*). Although after-the-fact and a bit theatrical, this image seeks to create a sense of the era's feverish climate. Woodcut after a painting by Georges Cain, 1881. Berlin, Archiv F. Kunst & Geschichte collection.

poking fun at the Revolution was forbidden. As a result, everything he owned was declared national property and confiscated – at four million livres, these were expensive songs indeed. The search also revealed evidence of 12,000 livres that he had left with Joseph, who was thus also in possession of national property. In the end, Jacques de Pelet was arrested (following another denunciation) and guillotined after a trial that was summary at best.

Joseph refused to back down, providing new papers and testimonies, writing to the heads of various dread committees, protesting prison conditions (his wife was pregnant at the time), demanding the services of a doctor, and even indicating where the money left with him by his father-in-law could be found in his home. Two officials came and took the money, but Joseph and his wife were left in prison, and she lost the child she was carrying.

They were set free in June 1794, as the period known as the Great Terror was beginning in Paris. They were in fact very lucky, as this phase of the Terror – marked by a mounting number of executions, most of them for specious or nonexistent reasons, and sometimes the result of denunciations motivated by nothing more than jealousy among neighbors – would surely not have spared them. The fall of Robespierre and his regime at the end of July, just a month and a half after Joseph was liberated, came as a great relief to them. From that time on, the former baron devoted himself exclusively to his vineyard.

Pichon's comeback

Unlike some vineyards, such as Lafite, Pichon-Longueville was not requisitioned by the Republic to

A Republican Beau. Created at the height of the Terror, this English depiction shows us the Jacobin revolutionary as he was imagined in London, a city closely linked to Bordeaux.
Colored engraving by Isaac Cruikshank, 1794.

provide wine to the soldiers. Its production, nonetheless, fell by half. For the five vintages of the Revolution, production dropped from an average of 62 casks to 32.

But in the long run, the Terror only briefly clouded Pichon-Longueville's brightest hours, and the vineyard quickly resumed its journey to greatness. In spite of the economic downturn experienced under the Directory, production increased to 36.8 casks in 1799. Under Bonaparte's government and then the Napoleonic Empire, it reached a record average of 83 casks, peaking at 115 casks in 1805 and 131 in 1808.

These figures, which are much higher than those from the years preceding the Revolution, show that extensive land purchases must have been made during the Revolution's first phase, as well as under the Directory. Joseph undoubtedly purchased church land confiscated by the state during the Revolution, but it is difficult to imagine that he would have acquired land confiscated from émigrés in the Revolution's second phase.

The economic crisis experienced under the Directory, however, resulted in many land sales. The liquid funds available to Joseph from his marriage allowed him to expand his estate. The Pichon-Lalande archive includes deeds of sale for collectively owned land or former collectively owned land put up for sale. This land often consisted of fields once farmed collectively by local peasants.

Pichon, the leading *troisième cru*

The vineyard's ascendance was not simply a question of volume. For the first time, Pichon-Longueville sold for *second cru* prices – not once but twice, in 1807 and 1814. A new official classification system, developed around 1815 by René Pijassou using William Lawton's archives, ranked it indisputably at the head of the *troisièmes crus*, just behind the *seconds crus*.

At that time, Joseph was on a fierce crusade to improve the quality of his wines and tried to align his prices with those of *seconds crus* like Léoville and Rauzan. Some years, he attempted to achieve these prices by selling late, a technique that did not always work. In 1815, William Lawton notably wrote that "Pichon-Longueville is generally robust and masculine, with good color and distinguished sap, albeit somewhat fat."

Joseph had become one of the richest and most prominent men in his region, and Napoleon, seeking to win over the provincial nobility and their broad local networks, attempted to curry favor with him. Joseph remained undecided until Napoleon's victory at Wagram and his marriage to Marie Louise of Austria. The Empire drifted further and further away from the Revolution – "les lys étouffent les abeilles," as it was said.* It seemed that Napoleon was a permanent fixture in the European political landscape. Joseph agreed to take on certain duties in the local government of Lesparre, where he had been imprisoned not long before.

Joseph and his wife had two daughters, Gabrielle, in 1795, and Virginie, in 1798, under the Directory.

A fervent supporter of the Bourbons

Destiny does not like excess. Napoleon had mastered Europe, but was limited by England's sea empire to the west and immense Russia to the east. He threw himself into conquering Russia, and his empire crumbled in a few months. Joseph's son, Raoul, was called up in a mass conscription intended to rebuild the army after its losses in Russia. He had himself declared unfit. Was his illness real? We cannot know, but he next appears in full military regalia on the back of a horse.

The French army was in disarray, fleeing on all fronts. In March 1814, the English reached the outskirts of Bordeaux, whose young nobles attempted to rally the forces to counter them. The city had suffered greatly from the continental blockade and remained in an economic depression that bordered on misery. With the Empire failing, Bordeaux took up arms for the Bourbons' return. Astride their horses, aristocrats like Raoul and his brother Louis from the region's winegrowing châteaux raised regiments and organized armed guards. Seized by romantic fervor, the young nobles gave all to experience the thrill of action.

The Duc d'Angoulême, nephew of Louis XVIII, and his wife, Louis XVI's daughter, were received in Bordeaux. Thereafter, Louis XVIII was brought back to the French throne, and Napoleon was exiled to the island of Elba. Rather infelicitously, the monarchy chose a white flag to represent itself.

When Napoleon returned, Louis XVIII fled, and Louis XVI's daughter sailed out of Bordeaux, escorted by Raoul. The humiliation of Waterloo and the second return of the Bourbons had come to naught, proving the fragility of things and the significance of France's other revolutionary half.

Still visible on this sword's blade is the engraved coat of arms of Louis XVIII (olive branches framing three French fleur-de-lys emblems). Could this have been the sword offered to Joseph by the king for the duke of Bordeaux's baptism?

Young men like Joseph's sons received military honors, but they were not politicians; rather, they were dreamers, nostalgic for the knights of yore. They never quite understood that the king could not snuff out the Revolution like an author crossing out an unsatisfactory passage in a novel. They were zealous servants of the monarchy, ultra-Royalists to the hilt.

More than epic battles, banners, and cannons, the Revolution had resulted in sweeping land transfers through the sale of national property – from which Pichon-Longueville had benefited. Barring another civil war, it would have been impossible to return to the way things had been: because of the great changes it had effected, the Revolution could not be undone. The Restoration was thus little more than a theater set, a sort of aborted historical reverie.

A Balzac novel

With five children reaching marriageable age, like the young people in Balzac's *Scenes from Private Life*, one might have thought that the family's future was secure. And it was, but for a fatal detail: it produced no descendants. To his great chagrin, Joseph lived to see the extinction of his family line.

Everything had begun so well. In recompense for his sons' sacrifices, the new regime named Joseph to the Bordeaux municipal council. He was invited to Paris in

* "The lilies are smothering the bees" – a reference to the emblem of the Bourbon monarchy, the lily, and that of Napoleon, the bee. Contemporaries often remarked that Napoleon had adopted the trappings of the monarchy, and that his royal aspirations had overrun his government's more republican pretensions.

1820 to represent his city at the christening of the heir to the throne, who had been named Duc de Bordeaux, and presented with a sword with a mother-of-pearl handle patterned with fleur-de-lys, which still hangs in the Château de Pichon-Lalande. His name was mentioned for the mayorship; his son Raoul followed in his father's footsteps up the social ladder. When his wife, Marguerite de Pelet, died in 1822, Joseph retired from political life – no matter, he must have thought; his son would take the reins.

Joseph's youngest child, Virginie, was married first, at 20, to the son of one of Bordeaux's most prestigious families, Comte Henri Raymond de Lalande. Soon after, Raoul married Virginie's sister-in-law. Sophie, the eldest, suffered in love and never married. Gabrielle married too late for any hope of issue. As for Louis, according to sources, he appears to have had little taste for women. After he took vows, his family obliged him to leave his orders to marry, but in vain. He rejected the many prospects presented to him.

In spite of this, some of the family's brightest hours were under the Restoration. Raoul, already mayor of Pauillac, was well on his way to replacing his father as mayor of Bordeaux, becoming a *pair**, and perhaps much more. Médoc high society spent many evenings at parties in the vineyards. One imagines the beautiful gowns, the fluttering fans, the Restoration-style coiffures, the languishing looks, the love affairs, the heartbreaks, the vividly moving, furious gallop of the music Rossini had made all the rage, the talk of the weather, the vintages, the great wines glowing like jewels in their glasses – wine that made such lavish expenditures possible with the dizzying prices it fetched in London. It recalls the balls and the devastating passions Balzac recounted in his novels of the provinces.

The 1830 Revolution in Paris broke across this idyll like a pistol shot ringing out in a ballroom. Charles X and his ultra-Royalists attempted to impinge on rights and advances established during the revolution. He was overthrown in a popular uprising and succeeded by a constitutional monarch. Raoul, a faithful and fervent** servant

to the Bourbons, refused to swear allegiance to Louis-Philippe, Philippe Égalité's son, who had voted to put Louis XVI to death, and stepped down from all his offices. The Pichon-Longueville family retreated from the political sphere.

At the same time, Virginie, who had been married for 12 years, had no children. Nor did Raoul, nor Gabrielle. Sophie had taken orders. Louis died soon after, in 1835.

Pichon-Longueville, *deuxième cru*

Despite the estate's larger surface area, production fell between 1815 and 1829 to levels not seen since before the Revolution. It dipped to 38 casks in 1816, and 30 casks the following year, averaging 65 casks per year, against the 83 casks produced under the Empire. People referred to 1816 as "the year without a summer" without understanding why. We now know that the Tambora, an Indonesian volcano, produced the largest explosion in recorded history in 1815, killing 12,000 people and propelling 80 cubic kilometers (19 cubic miles) of matter as far as the stratosphere. The finer dust particles remained in the atmosphere for months, creating a grayish veil that weakened the sun's rays.***

Wine production declined, but quality continued to improve. In 1815, Pichon-Longueville remained number one among *troisièmes crus* in the official classification based on William Lawton's archives.

Under the Restoration, two authors out of three named Pichon-Longueville a *second cru* based on tasting and market prices: Jullien, in his *Topographie de tous les vignobles connus***** in 1822, and Alexander Henderson,

* A pair was an honorific bestowed on notables since the time of Charlemagne. At the time, the title included membership in the High Legislative Assembly.
** Michel Figeac uses the very apt term *passionnel*, which means "passionate" in the sense of a passionate love, or a crime of passion.
*** *National Geographic* 159, no. 1 (January 1981); devoted to the explosion of Mount St. Helens.
**** Topography of All Known Wine Estates.

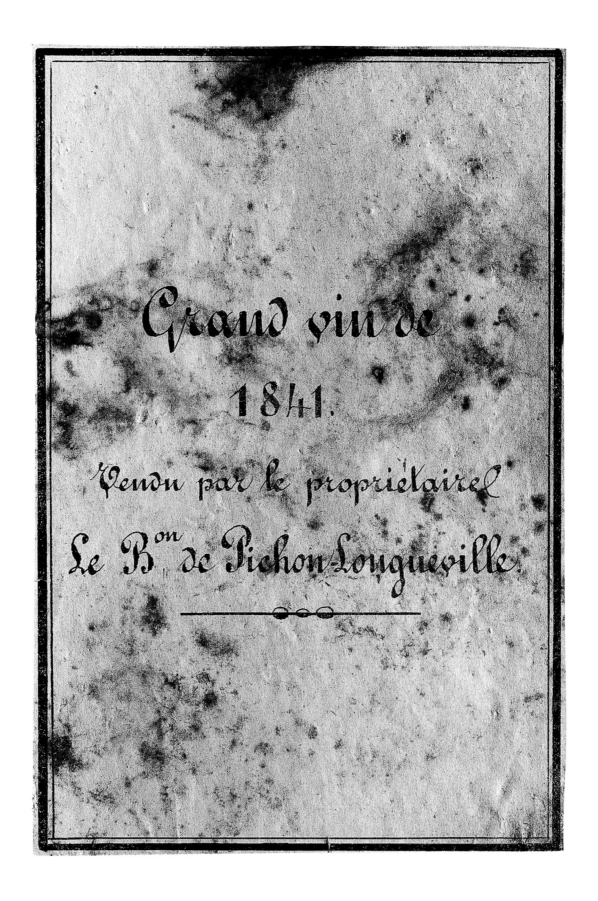

in his *History of Ancient and Modern Wines* in 1824. Only William Franck continued to rank the wine as a *troisième* in his *Traité sur les vins du Médoc et les autres vins rouges du département de la Gironde** in 1824. His conclusions were not heeded for long, and Pichon-Longueville took its place among the *seconds crus* under Louis-Philippe. The 1855 classification awarded a posthumous victory to Baron Joseph, and Pichon-Longueville was ranked *second cru* alongside Mouton, Cos d'Estournel, Léoville, Rauzan, Montrose, Ducru-Beaucaillou, and a few others.

The division and the two Pichons

In 70 years of work and through carefully calculated choices, Joseph had built a magnificent winegrowing estate, comprising 50 hectares (124 acres) of *second cru* vineyards, as well as heaths, fields, and forests. The absence of a single heir would not only end the Pichon-Longueville line, it would break up his life's work: the Revolution had instituted equal inheritance among descendants, regardless of birth order or sex.

Joseph died in December 1849 at the age of 90. He did all he could within the confines of the law to favor his oldest son, Raoul-Albert, leaving him his deceased brother Louis's share in the inheritance. The estate was divided into five shares to be distributed among the four living children. Thus, two of these shares, or 20 hectares (49 acres) were left to Raoul, while his sisters, Sophie, Gabrielle, and Virginie, each received ten hectares (24.5 acres).

24.5 acres was not enough to create a viable new estate. Whether it was practical reasons, friendship, rebellion, or all three that brought them together, Sophie, the eldest, and Virginie, Comtesse de Lalande, the youngest, created a lifelong partnership. Together, they created a 49-acre estate across from Raoul's. The two Châteaux Pichon-Longueville were born.

At first, all of the siblings made their wine at Raoul's, as he had inherited the house and the estate's only winemaking equipment. Virginie later built the Château de Pichon-Lalande, and then added the requisite winery and

cellar. Thus, starting in 1856, the two sisters were able to make their own Pichon-Lalande wine, while Gabrielle continued to use her brother's facilities. When he died in 1865, Gabrielle was widowed, blind, and ill. She left her land to her sister Virginie in 1875, making her estate the larger of the two. The three sisters were united symbolically in an estate across from the château of their two departed brothers, and Pichon-Longueville Comtesse de Lalande as we know it today was born.

* Treatise On Médoc Wines and Other Red Wines of the Gironde.

Le Baron Joseph de PICHON LONGUEVILLE   Page 74

— Admirez le teint frais de son propriétaire !..

Engraving from Biarnez's book (1849), which conjures both spiritual and humorous images of the Médoc's great wines.

Above: *Le port de Pauillac.* Oil on canvas, 1842.

Below: a map of 18th- century Médoc by cartographer
Pierre de Belleyme.

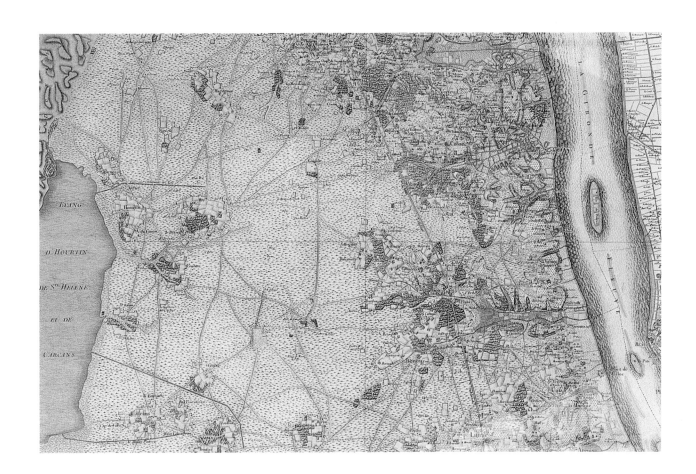

Left: Venetian glasses, 18th and 19th centuries. Pichon-Longueville Lalande Collection.
Right: glass receptacles, Rome, 1st century A.D.

Sophie and Virginie Founders of Pichon-Lalande (1856)

Sophie, Painter and Romantic (1785-1858)

If Sophie had not chosen to stand by her sister financially, ultimately leaving her everything she possessed, Pichon-Lalande would probably never have existed.

But the life of Sophie, Joseph's eldest daughter, remains a mystery. Yet these unknowns have the effect of making the personality she expressed in her painting and poetry even more endearing.

Her sensibilities are expressed very clearly in her artistic work. We know that she suffered, though we do not know exactly why. No documents from her or her siblings have been able to shed any light on the central mystery of her life. Only allusions and enigmatic images remain. There are few characters as unusual as Sophie in the history of the Médoc.

She left a body of artwork. In all, 14 paintings have been attributed to her, and a 15th may be a self-portrait. No doubt others once existed, but they are lost to us today, hidden away in an attic or hanging anonymously in someone's home. It is difficult to imagine, for example, that Sophie would have made a portrait of her brother-in-law, the Comte de Lalande, without painting one of her sister, Virginie, with whom she was so intimately connected.

A collection of poetry composed of 16 carefully ordered pieces and printed by the author also exists. The collection, entitled *Poésies fugitives* ("Fleeting Poems"), is printed on vellum watermarked with the coat of arms of Louis XVIII. The work, dedicated "to my mother, who always asked me for a collection of my verses," can therefore be dated after 1822, the year Marguerite de Narbonne-Pelet died. It could not have been published after 1823, when Sophie de Pichon-Longueville renounced earthly pleasures and became a canoness in the Order of Saint Anne in Würzburg, and then in Munich.

These poems evoke two traumatic events in the artist's life. The first was the Revolution, and the second involves a mysterious and sorrowful love affair. What transpired in the life of this woman of such romantic sensibilities?

Childhood and youth

Born in 1785, Sophie was Joseph's only child to have any memories of life before the Revolution. She was seven years old when her family fled Bordeaux for the Médoc, and she was eight and a half when her parents were arrested. Her ninth birthday present was their liberation from prison in June 1794. Her early childhood is thus marked by a feeling of paradise lost, of continual deterioration that led from happiness to despair. While her parents were in prison, a time that must have seemed interminable in her mind, she was put in charge, so to speak, of

her younger brothers, Raoul, who was born in 1787, and Louis, born in 1789. One can easily imagine how thrilled she must have been to get her parents back in June.

This first ordeal would mark her forever. She became passionately attached to the Bourbons when they returned to power. Four of the poems in her collection allude to the events of 1814 and the birth of the Duc de Bordeaux, the dynasty's great hope. One of these poems is dedicated to the daughter of Louis XVI, the Duchesse d'Angoulême, and another one of them was actually presented to her. The last line of the collection is addressed to God, and refers to the much-awaited birth of the Duc de Bordeaux: "Et guéris du passé la profonde blessure..."* This is France's past, but it is also her own.

We know very little about Sophie's childhood and adolescence. She received a very refined education and showed a remarkable talent for painting. We know that she was taught by a master in Bordeaux, but no information exists as to when or by whom. To have attained the mas-

tery she displays in an oil copy dated 1810 of her grandfather's portrait by Perroneau (p. 42), it is certain that she worked assiduously.

That same year, Joseph decided to take the Empire's side. Sophie's 1809 trip to attend a ball in Lesparre, in the northern part of the *département*, must be placed in this context. The journey as it is evoked in verse and prose shows a young (she was 24), lighthearted woman who enjoyed laughter. Her keen sense of observation, honed, no doubt, by drawing, did not miss a thing, whether ridiculous or touching.

Adressed to "Laure," a close friend, she recounts her journey "...in this carriage, which we might better call a cart, covered in a cloth pierced with small holes in the guise of windows. In vain, the eye sought out points of interest; there were none. The roads were very bad, and we bounced along from one jolt to another."

* "And heal this deep wound of the past..."

Finally, the travelers arrived "...at the much desired desti-nation. Small, low, poorly built houses, an old neglected church...were the only charms of this watering hole,"

That its dullard people
Called a city.

Sophie, who was very much the daughter of Baron Joseph, was quick to note the mannerisms of the canton's *nouveaux riches*. We are in the home of a Doctor Mongane:

"There was the ballroom. We dressed and went down; there we found violins, clarinets, all the music the neigh-borhood had to offer, to the great delight of the country's assembled beauties."

Elderly ladies I saw
In plentiful abundance;
Indeed, two or three, more wizened than the rest,
Surpassed all propriety.
One old crone – one of many!
With hobbled gait that passed for dancing,
Clattered about like a crippled grasshopper
To marvelous effect.
If only you had been there to share my mirth!
I could have burst, thinking of it.
For the sake of their pride,
I made due with a smile.
My neighbor was comical indeed
Dressed quite singularly,
In garb that drew from both
The Greek and Gothic styles
In a most particular fashion.

But not everyone there was ridiculous – grace might appear anywhere, and Sophie's gaze was generous. She noted "A small person... I never saw anyone so kind, ele-gantly dressed, a lovely dancer:"

She married charm and a delicate manner;
Gentle bearing, kindness;
An air of modesty with one of pleasure.
Her figure had a slender elegance,
And most of all, a thousand sweet gestures
Surpassed in grace the finest trappings she might have
worn.

Pouring rain delayed her return from Lesparre by a day. In a letter to the same Laure, Sophie confides in her, revealing something of her character:

My intent is not to flatter you,
One cannot know you without loving you.
Not as I myself do, I will add;
Not everyone loves as I love.

This depth of feeling would offer her both the best and the worst of life.

A pupil of Gérard

Sophie, armed with this depth of feeling and her prowess in painting, went to Paris with her father's blessing. She joined the studio of François Gérard, Napoleon's semi-official painter. Whether she studied painting in Paris before beginning in the painter's studio is unknown. In any case, she must have left for Paris, by a generous esti-mate, sometime between 1811 and 1813, as she executed a copy of a detail from Gérard's *Le Rêve d'Ossian* in his studio in 1814. That her father, who was highly indul-gent of her, allowed her to go and live the life of an artist is quite surprising for the period. We know, however, that Joseph was rather open-minded. She probably left for Paris before France's calamitous Russian retreat; it hardly seems likely that the Baron would send his daugh-ter to Paris if he had thought that the regime was wob-bling. Therefore, we may conclude that Sophie set off for the French capital in the spring of 1812 at the very latest, and very likely before that.

Once he had made a portrait of an earthly sovereign, French or otherwise – be it Napoleon, Marie-Louise, Czar Alexander, or Louis XVIII – Gérard* then had to provide a large number of reproductions for ministries, embassies, and consulates, where the painting hung in state. These orders were made "one after the other and in great haste," as one of his rare biographers put it.** He

* He was known as "the king of painters and the painter of kings."
** Adolphe Viollet-Leduc, in a long preface to *Correspondance de François Gérard*. Paris: Lainé et Havard, 1867.

François Gérard (1770-1837), *Ossian Evoking Ghosts on the Banks of the Lora with the Sound of His Harp.*
Oil on canvas, c. 1802. Malmaison, châteaux de Malmaison et Bois-Préau.

Partial copy, reinterpreted with brighter colors, by Sophie de Pichon-Longueville in 1814. With the Empire in ruins, what "ghosts" could be recalled here with such ardor, if not those of the Bourbons?

had a team composed primarily of young and talented women who were responsible for making these many copies. Sophie must have honed her craft by reproducing these official paintings. She worked alongside other young women like her, including Gérard's first assistant, Mademoiselle Godefroid, who left recollections and portraits of the master.

Sophie executed the copy of a detail from *Ossian évoque les fantômes au son de la harpe*, signed and dated 1814, having immersed herself in the exalted atmosphere of James Macpherson's poem. After the artificial landscapes and pastoral scenes so popular in 18th century France, the Poems of Ossian contributed to the beginnings of a sea change in European sensibilities. More and more, this new, romantic taste sought raging torrents, harsh mountain landscapes, nightscapes, impetuous feelings, consuming passions, and unbounded love. Sophie, whom we know was capable of the latter, threw herself wholeheartedly into this new trend. Her paintings are an eloquent illustration of this.

Sophie was a great follower of Rousseau. She loved books, and built up a sizeable library for herself. She read his *Confessions* as well as *La Nouvelle Héloïse*, which was an immense success in the provinces and revealed an extensive audience of female readers. Following the *Songe d'Ossian*, Sophie threw herself into painting mountain landscapes. We are reminded of Rousseau's words: "It is already understood what I mean by a fine country; never can a flat one, though ever so beautiful, appear such in my eyes: I must have torrents, fir trees, black woods, mountains to climb or descend, and rugged roads with precipices on either side to alarm me."*
Sophie was a child of the flatlands, raised in the Médoc and Bordeaux, but she lived by this maxim.

A devastating passion

Gérard's salons were at least as celebrated as his studio, frequented by all of the period's great names. Would Sophie have been invited to them? It is more than likely. It was perhaps there that she met a young man from the Savoy, with whom she fell madly in love. 1814 and the following year were a time of astonishing reversals: the fall of the Empire, the return of the Bourbons, the Hundred Days, the Bourbons' second return. A parallel may be drawn between this charged atmosphere and a painting of the poet Ossian on the banks of the Lora in a mountainous landscape, evoking ghosts as if to call them forth. It is quite possible that Sophie was thinking of the call for the Bourbons' return when she painted this picture. We do know that her life's most fateful moments took place during these hectic years; we know it was then that she lived a devastating passion. Yet again, history and her personal destiny intertwined.

We know that she went to take the waters at Vichy in 1814; she writes about the experience in her collection of poetry. She then went to Bordeaux, where she met the Duchesse d'Angoulême, daughter of Louis XVI.

And then what? Most likely, she traveled to meet her beloved in the Alps, near the Saint Gothard pass. Was this before 1815 or after? The mountain landscapes she painted were almost certainly executed from sketches she made herself. The topographical precision noted by Swiss friends of Pichon-Lalande cannot lie. Was it there that she lived out her great love, at the age of 30, and then the terrible break that followed? This, at least, is what she seems to be telling us in these mountain scenes.

This mysterious, bespectacled young man was either Savoyard or Italian. He was very likely the thwarted, lost, or "impossible" love of our painter.

* *The Confessions of Jean-Jacques Rousseau*, Book IV.

Two diptych Alpine landscapes by Sophie, 1820-1821.
Before. A woman in a white dress, probably Sophie, sketches beside her bespectacled lover as he looks on. In a time of betrothal and happy promise, the water, like the road to the right, is calm.

After. A black-clad woman turns away from a uniformed man holding a horse with a sidesaddle. Now, in a time of grief, isolation, inner torment, even death, the river rages, shattering tree trunks and crashing against the rocks. The perilous road crosses over the angry torrent via the Pont du Diable, identified by Swiss friends of Pichon-Lalande.

Did she return to Paris in the following years, between 1816 and 1819? As noted above, Joseph was charged with representing Bordeaux to the king on the occasion of the Duc de Bordeaux's christening in 1820. We know he received a sword decorated with the arms of Louis XVIII. Had she been in the capital at the time, Sophie may have been invited, before her definitive return to Aquitaine with her father. Whatever may have been the case, we know that she was in the Médoc or in Bordeaux roughly between 1820 and 1821, because it was then that she painted the handsome portrait of her brother-in-law, Comte Henri Raymond de Lalande, Virginie's husband, as well as two mountain scenes. All of these are dated between 1820 and 1821.

The documents available to us tell us much about Sophie's sensibilities, as well as the general state of her emotions, but offer little detail. One comes away with the impression that she must have taken great care to destroy anything that might reveal her secret.

A portrait exists of the mysterious, bespectacled young man who appears in her mountain scenes. At Pichon-Lalande, he was simply known as "Sophie's fiancé," but we do not know who he was. Oddly, he wears a small tricolor flag in his buttonhole. There is enough resemblance, particularly in the hair and glasses, to leave little doubt that the picture represents the same person we see in the Alps with Sophie. He looks proud, sure of himself, and sure of what he thinks. We do not know when Sophie painted this portrait.

What are these pictures trying to tell us? What kind of riddle is Sophie inviting us to solve? The symbolism in the mountain scenes is clear: the white dress recalls marriage,

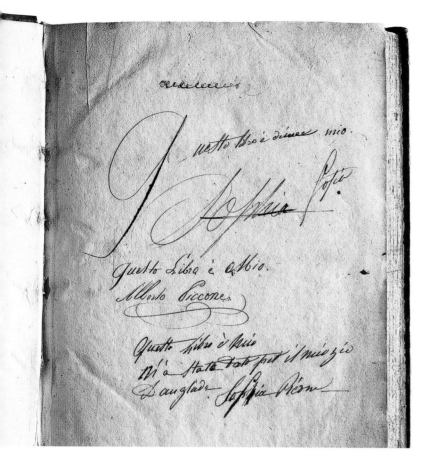

love, springtime, happy promise; the black dress by the Pont du Diable evokes mourning. The man in uniform is holding her horse, as she is seated sidesaddle on it. If he was a cavalry officer, where is his own horse? Why doesn't it appear in the painting? His uniform leads us to believe that he may have been mobilized, and is leaving the young woman, who cannot accept the situation, to go to war.

A piece in Sophie's collected poetry entitled *Idylle* notes that it was "composed upon receiving a proposal of marriage while in a foreign country." It sheds a sliver of light on her saga:

Little birds, how your song
Is bittersweet!
Your only sadness
Is in the absence of springtime
You alone taste the sweetness of friendship,
with no thought for its loss.

You love without shedding tears,
With no fear of fate.
To leave a friend, a beloved mother,
For you holds no terror,
You do not know of these torments.
Oh, if you but knew of my sad fate!
Little birds, can you wonder
That I find you joyful?
Stop your singing! But why prevent you?
Let the echoes ring out;
Sing, birds, sing of my complaint
Your silence would only amplify my sorrow.

Sophie owned an Italian dictionary, which bears her signature and a few words of Italian written in her hand. Other books, also in Italian, contain handwritten vocabulary notes with words and their French translations. Might she have refused a marriage proposal in order to remain with her mother? Her mother may have been ill at the time – we know that she passed away the year after Sophie painted these mountain scenes.

Another piece, called *Romance*, gives new clues:

In a castle on the Isère's banks,
There lived a gentle troubadour
Each morning saw the poet pray
That crafty god men call Amour.
That my Elmire and I, he sighed,
Be touched by your bright fire,
That I my love might tell to her!
Loving alone is too harsh a fate.

For her part, a shepherdess,
Called upon that selfsame god.
Oh! If he loved me! Oh! If he were true,
Nothing could equal my devotion.
It would last as long as the light;
It would shine from my eyes
Even as Death closed them,
Its memory would follow me to the gods.

His lovely fingers moved across the lyre

Playing the chords his heart drew from them:
The god was touched. On his empire, he swore
Joy to the maiden and the troubadour
In the temple of marriage, he sealed their troth
Bedecked them with flowers, lifelong love;
Then to gentle Hymen the flame he passed.

But the happy denouement to this poem is just a dream, an illusion, cruelly shattered in the following poem, which is called *Le songe d'une mere* ("Dream of a Mother"). The brutal contrast between the two is clearly intentional.

Alas! I awake, and must
Lose you once again!
Day dawns; it blots away
The error of my slumbers.
Tonight, you were returned to me;
I pressed you to my heart –
In my joy, I believed
You had never been lost from me.
[...]
Often, in its plaintive chords,
My lyre calls you from the abyss
Often, too, full of thoughts of you,
I follow you in dense woods;
I seek you in the valley;
I see you! ...you have flown!
The wind shivers and sighs;
It quickens my delirium.
Can I hear you?
To my battered soul,
Everything recalls you.
In this land of exile,
Nothing remains for me
Or my abandoned sorrow,
But death.

This poem, reproduced here in part, evokes Sophie's suffering. As a poet, she was certainly no match for Lamartine, or, a bit later, the young Victor Hugo. Then

Left: bookplate in Italian with the signatures of Sophie and a mysterious Alberto Piccones. The young bespectacled man?

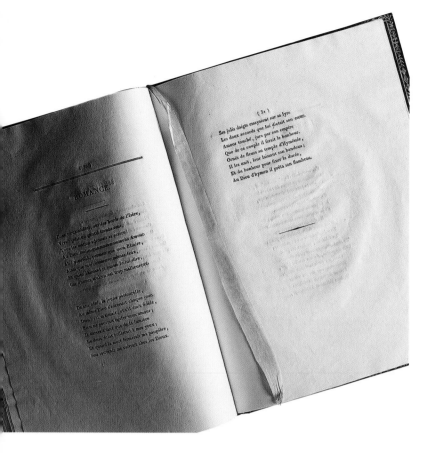

A heartfelt cry indeed. Sophie's poems do not mention any betrayal on the part of her beloved. If, then, we exclude this eventuality, we are left with only two hypotheses. Either her beloved died at war (at Waterloo or elsewhere), or it was Sophie who broke off their engagement. Perhaps she chose not to exile herself from Bordeaux, to leave her family or an ailing mother. With her family fervently loyal to the Bourbons, perhaps she felt too much distance between herself and a young man fired with the legacy of the Revolution and the Empire, and proud of his convictions. Could the little tricolor flag in his buttonhole be a key to the enigma? It certainly isn't the white Bourbon flag with its fleur-de-lys that her brothers wore on their arms like a blazon of glory. The collection's insistence on the return of the Bourbons, her love for the Duchesse d'Angoulême, the hope placed in the birth of the Duc de Bordeaux – all these should be lined up against this mysterious tricolor insignia in the buttonhole of the man she loved and painted. Was Sophie, true to her intense and imaginative spirit, seeking an impossible situation, an impossible love affair? This may not lie far from the truth.

again, French Romantic poetry was just beginning to emerge in 1823. In any case, Sophie's utter sincerity is palpable and moving. The poem's tension is real, even if it does lack an element of daring and would be better off with an aesthetic less immersed in the past.

Sophie had no known children; the image in this elegy is a transposed one, recalling a lost love. But while her infinite suffering is abundantly clear, its exact cause remains indistinct. *Sur la campagne* ("In the Countryside") speaks volumes.

Flow by, my days; may the placid brook
Be muddier, and more restless than you!
Fly, oh pleasures, fly city uproar:
You are more brilliant, more lively, but far less sweet.
And you, my heart, in this exile, keep,
If you may, a constant peace,
And for your happiness – alas! – never love!

The retreat

Following the death of her mother in 1822, Sophie collected her poems and had them printed. These "fugitive poems" were published with an *Invocation aux songes*, an invocation to the dreams in which she first took refuge.

Come, sweet dreams,
Sleep's companions;
Wrap us in your pleasant lies;
Leave us only when we wake...

She executed other paintings, including *Roland à Roncevaux*, another mountain scene, this time on the theme of friendship, and then decided to retire. In 1823, she became an honorary member of the Congregation of Sisters of Saint Anne in Würzburg. As this convent was

Above: *Roland et Olivier à Roncevaux* (*Roland and Olivier at Roncevaux*).
Below: *Le Christ et les marchands du Temple* (*Jesus and the Money Changers in the Temple*).

attached to one in Munich, she was a lady of honor in the Munich convent until her death in 1858.

It should be noted that this lay status had to be purchased. The habit, which she had the right to wear in her travels through Europe, offered her protection and freedom.

But the status was more than just a safe passage. In the Pichon-Longueville tradition, Sophie had chosen to follow a spiritual path that would finish with a truly mystical oeuvre. She wrote no more poems – at least, none known to us today – and painted religious subjects like

the *Christ en croix* ("Christ on the Cross") in the Pauillac church. A remarkable sketch, *Le Christ et les vendeurs du Temple* ("Christ Driving the Merchants from the Temple"), recalls Géricault. She painted portraits of Saint James and Saint Peter, and *L'enfant au col du Grand Saint-Bernard* ("Child and Saint Bernard"). She also executed two landscape paintings of the Geneva area. In them, though the mountains tower in the background, the water in the foreground is still at last. These luminous landscapes recall the paintings of the Italian *vedutisti*. Sophie's work shows that she traveled extensively throughout Europe, returning to the Alps to paint – and perhaps to create an artistic break with her youth. Books bearing Sophie's signature were purchased in Bagnères-de-Luchon – the Pyrénées, more mountains.

A self-portrait?

A final enigma remains, that of a portrait that once hung in Pichon-Baron, and was sold when Raoul-Albert de Pichon-Longueville's estate was dispersed. The painting was later reacquired by Madame de Lencquesaing, who looks out for anything relating to Pichon's history. Numerous clues suggest it is Sophie's self-portrait, painted when she was a lady of honor in the congregation. First, the melancholy expression of the model, whom the painter does not flatter, is uncommon in an ordinary portrait. It is difficult to imagine a subject agreeing to be portrayed in this manner. Second, and more important, the black velvet dress is the habit worn by this congregation, with a 75-millimeter flame-colored ribbon striped with silver descending from the left shoulder to the right hip. A pink ribbon of the same width worn around the neck seems to be a detail used by the painter to brighten the work, unless an unknown rule called for it. The face shows no signs of rouge or other makeup, and does not seem to have been touched up at all, as befitted a religious woman. This dedication to absolute truth shows in Sophie's artistic – and religious – approach. Finally, the subject shows a striking resem-

Vue d'un lac de montagne en Suisse (*View of a Mountain Lake in Switzerland*).

blance to Virginie and Joseph; the shape of the nose and mouth seem typical of the Pichon-Longueville family. If Sophie painted this portrait toward the end of the 1820s, or later, she would have been around 40, perhaps older. The model's inclined neck and head seem to say, "I did what I could," in a sign of fragility, of a soft feminine character. Renowned Italian playwright Valeria Moretti provides us with another clue in her *Le più belle del reale*. The text looks at the work of women through history who dedicated themselves to painting, and struggled to build careers for themselves when such a choice was nearly inconceivable for a woman. Looking at women painters, including Sophonisba Anguissola in Cremona, Elisabetta Sirani in Bologna, Artemisia Gentileschi in Naples, and Elisabeth Vigée-Lebrun in Paris, Moretti shows us that, for these women, the self-portrait was a sort of right of entry to the masculine world of painting – a sort of proof of these women painters' existence. In an interview with us, Moretti explained that it is highly improbable that a woman like Sophie would not have left a self-portrait, like a woman's private diary. But there is one difference between Sophie and the women painters Moretti studied. These other women managed to make painting their profession, often selling their work for very hefty prices, whereas Sophie supported her painting and poetry herself – hence the absence of the flattering mask Moretti's painters often used to assert themselves in a men's world. Sophie used no such mask. Though she was paid by Gérard for her reproductions, there are no other known sales of her work. Perhaps her broken love affair changed things for her, ending a promising career.

A talent never fully realized?

Sophie showed surprising aptitude to excel in a wide variety of styles. In its composition, its colors, its expressions, and the authenticity of its inspiration, *Christ et les marchands du Temple*, painted in the spirit of Géricault and Delacroix, clearly shows that she was very much in tune with her era's trends.

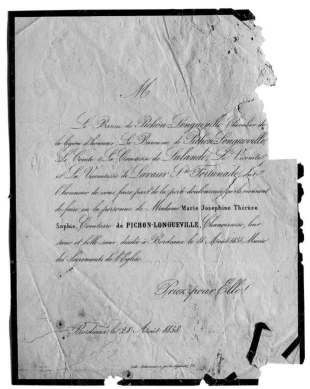

Above: Caspar David Friedrich (1774-1840), *Wanderer Above the Sea of Clouds.* Oil on canvas, 1818. Hambourg, Kunsthalle.
Above right: The comtesse Sophie de Pichon-Longueville's death announcement.

Her use of landscape to bring personal drama to life indicates that she became aware of the era's sensibilities quite early. Swiss painters François Diday (1802-1877) and Alexandre Calame (1810-1864), who came after Sophie, glorified the force or serenity of their landscapes, but did not include human passions and all they evoked in their work. Pierre de la Rive (1753-1817) remained an 18th-century genre painter. Sophie's painting style may only really be compared with that of Caspar David Friedrich (1774-1840), of whom the sculptor David d'Angers said, "He has discovered the tragedy of landscape." The German painter, who regained prominence in the 20th century, was a master at creating harmony between one or several personas and landscapes that evoked an interior drama, or emotion. But Friedrich never came to Paris; he was trained in Copenhagen and chose to stay in Dresden. Did Sophie ever meet this highly original painter? It is unlikely; the life path she chose, without ever attempting to gain renown, was probably simply her own.

If she had been a man, her life would certainly have been different. Her place as a woman in a world that offered her little room to become an artist no doubt stifled her. Would true liberty have allowed her to pursue her art as far as it could take her? No one can say. Her paintings, with their myriad styles, show that she explored a number of artistic paths. And if nothing else, she, along with her sister, contributed to the creation of Pichon-Lalande, a praiseworthy accomplishment indeed.

Sophie died in 1858 at the age of 73, leaving a will. In it, she made several gifts to charitable works, and left her portion of their inheritance and all her fortune to her younger sister. Today, her body of work forms an outstanding collection attached to the Château Pichon-Longueville Comtesse de Lalande.

Virginie, Comtesse de Lalande (1798-1882)

The woman who gave the château its name belonged firmly to the new world born of the Revolution – she was just a year old when Napoleon took power, and she knew of the perils her parents lived through only by word of mouth.

A beautiful woman

Virginie had no particular talent for painting or writing. According to contemporary documents and correspondence, Virginie's most noteworthy trait was her great beauty. She no doubt combined this with grace and charm, as she drew many admirers throughout her life. She had a hot temper and a strong character, and she showed them often. Perrignon's famous portrait of her, which has become the emblem of the Château Pichon-Lalande, are testament to her radiant beauty. The painting, made when she was no less than 60, reveals a dramatic tension. Though as a portrait it was no doubt painted to flatter its subject, it could not lie about the structure of her face, the harmony of the features, and her charming gaze.

It is therefore unsurprising that, though she was the youngest of Joseph's children, she was the first to marry, at the age of 20, in 1818. She married Charles Henri, Comte Raymond de Lalande, who was then 30. Perhaps they were introduced to one another at one of the many parties given at Pichon-Longueville or in Bordeaux, when her family was at the height of its influence. One can only imagine that numerous men vied for such a woman; endowed with youth, beauty, riches, and good breeding, she had her pick of suitors. The Comte de Lalande, painted by Sophie in 1823, was a handsome man, with a seemingly gentle character. He has a certain discreet amusement in his gaze that seems to mix humor and fancy.

Left: Virginie de Pichon-Longueville, comtesse de Lalande, by Perrignon, in 1858, her sixtieth year, in mourning for her sister.
Above: Her husband, Henri comte Raymond de Lalande, by Sophie de Pichon-Longueville, in 1823.

We may therefore assume that Virginie was in love with her husband, and what follows confirms this. Charles Henri Raymond de Lalande came from one of the wealthiest families in Bordeaux before the Revolution, and one of the most brilliant and refined as well.

The Lalande family

Though it did not produce any heirs, the Lalande family's alliance with the Pichon-Longuevilles, who typically embraced a shrewd matrimonial strategy, was a logical one. The Lalandes came from Beautiran. As was fitting of their station, they had been members of the *parlement* under the Ancien Régime. They had invested in triangular trade in Santo Domingo, and rapidly built up a large fortune dealing in sugar, coffee, and slaves. Their palatial home, the Hôtel de Lalande, was designed by the archi-

tect Laclotte and furnished in a princely fashion. Their sumptuous parties were known for the best music Bordeaux high society had to offer.

The city's prestige, architectural beauty, and extravagance attracted France's greatest talents. The Duc de Richelieu, who governed the province, stopped at nothing to ensure the surpassing splendor of his region – considered excessive by some. The municipal magistrates complained of the cost, but singers, actors, musicians, and dancers flocked to Bordeaux. Even the great Molé gladly left the Comédie-Française to perform in its marvelous theater, Victor Louis's masterpiece. The dancer Dauberval and his wife, Madame Théodore, who were attached to Bordeaux, were ranked among France's greatest choreographers. Evenings at the Hôtel de Lalande reflected all this artistic and cultural glory.

The Revolution came down hard on this highly – all too highly – prominent family. Jean de Lalande was guillotined in 1793, after a cursory trial. His son, Virginie's future husband, was just five years old. Their home was declared national property by the Revolution and was confiscated; its heirs were never able to recover it. The Château de Beautiran was burned. The fortune the family had built up in Santo Domingo was swept away by the rising tide of political events and wars, including slavery's abolition, Toussaint Louverture's government, and Haitian independence, won in 1804 after a heated war against the troops sent by Napoleon Bonaparte to reinstate slavery. Today, the Hôtel de Lalande houses the Bordeaux Museum of Decorative Arts.

Virginie and Charles Henri were married in 1818, and the two families further consolidated their alliance a year later, when Raoul-Albert de Pichon-Longueville married Charles Henri's younger sister, Marie-Armande. Thus, two Pichon siblings married two Lalande siblings. Neither couple produced any offspring.

Sterility and a history of mentalities

From the time of their weddings to the first part of the 20th century, the word "sterility" by definition only applied to women. It was not until Hotchkiss's work in 1943 that the idea of male sterility appeared. Today, we know that sterility in couples is statistically even between the two sexes. But in the 19th century, sterility was seen as an exclusively female problem. In its 1879 edition, the *Grande Encyclopédie Larousse* puts it this way: "At times, the absence of children in a marriage is due to the man's impotence, but this is the rarest of cases. Nine times out of ten, it is the woman who is unfit for childbearing."

As neither marriage was annulled (the Church granted annulments in cases of impotence), we can only conclude that the two couples were without issue for biological reasons that were intractable in the 19th century. As the two couples were from the same generation and the same families, it is impossible to know the origin of their sterility. What we do know, and what is important to this his-

tory, is that given the prejudices of the period, Virginie certainly felt guilty and responsible for this situation. As for Raoul-Albert, his misogyny, which he expressed more than once, may speak for him in this matter.

Virginie must have endured a long period of deep suffering. During it, her understanding of her own destiny,

and that of her husband's, to whom she could not "give" a baby, must have changed. After so many infertile years, we make out a hint of worry, then spiritual anguish, tears, a kind of fragility, and finally, certainty. And then, another kind of love takes root, grows, and turns exclusively toward her husband; Virginie seems to have experienced it as a sort of debt to him. But this same situation was also what led her to devote all her energy to the great wine under her care. Her actions cannot be separated from this analysis of her marriage and its psychological consequences.

The powdery mildew crisis

When Joseph's estate was divided among his children in 1850, Raoul ceded a part of his land (compensated elsewhere) to his sisters for construction. It was located near the road, in Petit Bois. As soon as she had received Sophie's support and was certain that she would be overseeing a 49-acre estate equal to Raoul's, Sophie had the Château of Pichon-Lalande built. It was designed by architect Henri Duphot. A winery and cellar followed in 1856, the first year that Sophie and Virginie made their own wine separately from their brother.

Such major investments required a period of continued prosperity. That was not, however, what the future had in store. Virginie's beginnings in winemaking coincided with the powdery mildew crisis.

As Bruno Prats, who headed the Cos d'Estournel for nearly 30 years, put it, "Up to the mid-19th century, the grapevine experienced a golden age when it was not touched by disease – at least the major destructive diseases." The grapevine's everyday enemy was the snail. These pests were easily kept at bay by the winemakers' wives, who walked through the vineyards collecting them in buckets. They filled up rapidly in damp periods, as we read in the Pichon-Lalande archives.

When powdery mildew arrived from London's greenhouses, tore through Belgium, and then through Paris and its surrounding cities, the wine world was unprepared. Powdery mildew was called *la maladie de la vigne*, or vine sickness, as it was the only one anyone had ever seen at the time. The mildew was the first cryptogamic disease to strike before the terrible downy mildew crisis that swept the Médoc 30 years later. It spread rapidly and without stopping. Its presence and the great damages it wreaked were recorded starting in the summer of 1852 in the Pauillac appellation.

The summer of 1853 was a very rainy one. The grapes were attacked by rot, and harvest volumes plummeted. Between 1852 and 1858, they dropped an average of 75%. Virginie and Sophie, who had already started work on the château and then the winery and cellar, harvested 12 acres of the 49 they possessed. Financial difficulties loomed.

It took a long time to understand the crisis, and even more time to act. Some people believed that it was caused by an insect and others tried miracle cures, all to no avail. Still others cut their grapes from the vine and threw them into the Garonne river, thinking that they could stop the disease from propagating. The authorities offered a prize to anyone who discovered a solution to the problem, and hundreds of fantastical remedies circulated as a result. People tried fumigation, washing the grapes in ashes diluted in water, lime water, etc. Finally, one visionary man, a Monsieur Duchâtel de Château Lagrange, in Saint-Julien, discovered that he could spray his vines with powdered sulfur.

The idea of using sulfur on grapes was not terribly surprising – it was already used to sterilize barrels before filling them; one might say it was the easiest approach. The real question was how to apply it, when, and how to spray it without harming the health of the vine workers. It took a long time for the process to be put into wide use, as people feared that the sulfur's taste would show up in the wine. Often, estate owners did nothing, in the hopes that the disease would simply go away. It took some time for people to understand that time was powerless to eradicate it. Currently, genetics is the only possibility for avoiding disease treatment. This will most certainly spark debates analogous to those that took place centuries ago.

Little by little, sulfur overcame the crisis. And, as comparative tasting showed, it did not in fact alter the wine's taste. Monsieur Duchâtel's solutions were widely adopted. The first large-scale trials took place in 1860, and in 1861, it was decided that sulfuring should be done annually. In 1863, preventive sulfuring became common. These treatments, of course, made the return on investment for a grape on the vine much steeper.

The paradox of these years is that, while there was real worry in the wine world, there was no desperate reaction to the crisis. The sale price of a cask at the beginning of the powdery mildew crisis rose to entirely new heights, and did not waver for the next 30 years. This popularity may be explained by a number of factors: the fall in production; the rareness of Médoc wines, the absence of any alternative drink of the same caliber; the market's growth due to prosperity under the Second Empire; the building of railroads, which meant that Bordeaux wines could finally be obtained in Paris with relative ease and gave Parisians a taste for them; and the fashion sparked by the 1855 ranking.

The price per cask of certain *premiers crus* exceeded 5,000 francs in some years, and *seconds crus* like Pichon-Longueville sold for up to 3,000 francs or more in 1854. For the sake of comparison, let us recall that in the dark years that followed the phylloxera and the downy mildew crises, Pichon-Lalande sold with difficulty at 600 francs per cask in 1900, one of its greatest vintages of all times. And this a half a century later, in spite of a sharp rise in expenses and an overall rise in prices.

But even with the sale price so high, the vineyard was producing at only 25% capacity. The estate, and therefore Virginie, was struggling to survive in this era of heavy investments. Sophie's death in the summer of 1858 was a blow to her spirits. That year, the Comte de Lalande turned 70, and Virginie turned 60. Like the ladies of the vine in the 18th century, she looked after everything, coming to Pichon regularly to deal with the estate steward and the architect. But funds were cruelly lacking.

Virginia's inheritance from her sister granted her a second wind in the months following Sophie's death.

château, the winery, the cellar, and the equipment. She turned to less costly ways of furnishing the château than those of which she had originally dreamed.

The cost of building the château, which was designed by Henri Duphot, is unknown. For an idea of the financial difficulties Virginie had to surmount to complete it, it may be recalled that the Chatêau Latour, built by the same architect in the same period, was much smaller and less ambitious than Virginie's. It cost 45,000 francs. The price of the Pichon-Lalande château must have come to at least one and a half times as much, or some 60,000 francs. Add to that the cost of the winery, the cellar, the winemaking materials, and the château's furnishings, and we see that 80,000 francs was not very much to pay off the debt, with interest.

1858 is therefore a significant year in the life of the Comtesse de Lalande. It was also the year she had her portrait painted by Perrignon. Dressed in a black shawl, she sits against a gray background set off by pale rose pink, creating a harmony that evokes Goya's portraiture. The beauty of her face, even if it was enhanced (which is not certain), of her neck and shoulders, and of her hands, which are prominently shown, does not conceal the melancholy in her expression. The choice of black recalls mourning. Virginie had lost Sophie, one of the people she loved most in the world, and who had given her so much help in realizing her dream of making this unforgettable wine. Embodied in her paintings, Sophie became an object of much veneration at Pichon-Lalande. Once the powdery mildew crisis had passed, a tide of prosperity returned, carrying the countess and her wine with it. In 1875, upon the death of her sister Gabrielle, Virginie came into possession of her part in their father's estate. This famous vintage was the first from the three Pichon-Longueville sisters together. These were years of great fortune. Virginie oversaw the shipping of her great wine to Amsterdam, London, and Moscow.

And what of the other Pichon, Raoul's Pichon? Virginie was its natural heiress, given that she was much younger than her brother. Would she be able to bring the two parts of Joseph's vineyard back together?

Sophie had inherited half of the beautiful Hôtel Montméjean, the Pichon-Longueville family home in Bordeaux, from her father Joseph, who had left the other half to Gabrielle. In November 1858, Virginie sold Sophie's half to Gabrielle. The sale provided Virginie with 80,000 francs, enough to pay for the building of the

Pichon-Baron

Raoul-Albert was still alive in the beginning of 1864. At that time, both Louis and Sophie had died, and Gabrielle was ill and nearly blind. Raoul found himself living with his younger sister on the other side of the road – the two châteaux, after all, had been built facing each other, or very nearly so. Raoul was 77, Virginie 66. But Raoul was loath to let his vineyard fall into the hands of the last of the Pichon-Longuevilles.

Raoul was a passionate genealogist and a Legitimist. He wrote a sonnet against women for a Bordeaux charitable society, and then another in favor of them, condemning the first (perhaps following some recriminations from the women he frequented). He had a remarkable palate and was an ardent royalist, offering his home as a refuge to Carlos of Spain before he attempted to take back the throne. It is thus unsurprising that he decided to pass the Château Pichon-Baron on to a male heir of the Pichon-Parempuyre branch of the family, on the condition that the heir be adopted by him in due form.

As already mentioned, Bernard de Pichon, the man of the Fronde, had two sons. The eldest founded the Pichon-Parempuyre branch of the family, and the youngest, Jacques-François, created the Pichon-Longueville branch, which went on to have a more brilliant destiny than that of the elder brother.

The Pichon-Longuevilles, with no male family member capable of producing an heir in 1860, risked extinction, and on the eve of his death, Raoul-Albert decided to adopt a distant relation, a descendant of the elder brother's family line, which was not lacking in male heirs. He found a 26-year-old cousin, fittingly also named Raoul, who did not have to be asked twice to become the Baron de Pichon-Longueville's adopted son and heir.

The process was a race against time: Raoul-Albert was rapidly nearing the end of his life, growing weaker by the day. The adoption was carried out in August 1864, but that did not suffice in and of itself. The young man had to marry and produce an heir to ensure the family line would continue. On September 6th, he married Nathalie de Chanceaulme de Clarens; on August 14th, 1865, she gave birth to a son, who, naturally, was named Albert de Pichon-Longueville. Raoul-Albert had just enough time to see the new heir, dying just three weeks later at the end of September, satisfied that he had dutifully bequeathed his name, title, and château to its rightful heir, at least in his eyes. Thus ended the life of Raoul-Albert, yet another of our history's romantic characters, so typical of one facet of the French nobility after the Revolution.

Baron Raoul-Albert de Pichon-Longueville shortly before his death. He created the Pichon-Longueville Baron *cru*.

91

One can see here that the Château de Pichon-Lalande is directly
inspired by the Hôtel de Lalande in Bordeaux, built by Laclotte
in 1781. Apart from the central double staircase entrance,
the façade is a near replica of the Bordeaux *hôtel*.

It is far from certain that Virginie was delighted by this decision. Feeling abandoned by an older brother one looks up to, whatever the reasons, is never a pleasant sensation. Nothing remains, however, that might shed light on any party's feelings about the matter. If Virginie had once hoped to reunite the two estates under her name as the ultimate heiress, her brother's decision to perpetuate their family name marked the definitive separation of the two vineyards, which would henceforth each live out their own histories.

The Comtesse's château and its message

The château is a refined residence inspired by the Hôtel de Lalande in Bordeaux, with features designed to meet the demands of country living. Placing the spiral staircase in a tower on the château's rear facade opened up an extra room on each floor of the building, adding to its spaciousness. This pepperpot turret is a delicate nod to the architecture of the Middle Ages, while other elements recall the Renaissance or the 17th century. The Comtesse's château stands out for its good taste. It shows no vulgarity; nothing is out of place. It finds its balance in a style inspired by Bordeaux's architectural classicism. As the château of a Médoc wine estate, the building is intended to reflect the fine tradition of French nobility, identifying it with France's greatness from the Middle Ages to the Restoration. Michel Figeac has shown how these aristocrats, having lost their power following the Revolution, attempted to prove at every turn what their world and class were capable of: a search for absolute perfection and scorn for the quick profit so dear to the bourgeois class that had taken power.

Grand cru vineyards, which lived up to their full potential through patient cultivation and careful wine production over many centuries, were a way for these aristocrats to create a positive image of themselves. It was thus vital to have a home that expressed this concept in its very stones, for all eternity. The role of the château on the Pichon-Lalande estate was to embody the challenge of producing a timeless, high-quality wine despite the yearly inevitability of erratic weather.

Finally, on a more personal level, by making the Hôtel de Lalande the inspiration for the château, Virginie created a natural link between the Lalande and Pichon-Longueville names. This shows Virginie's desire to offer a legacy to her husband she could not provide through childbirth. Louis d'Estournel died in January 1853 without an heir, leaving his name to his château, the Cos d'Estournel. The Rauzans had done the same with their own château in the Margaux appellation. Such examples speak for themselves. Virginie hoped to make her husband's name live on in time, as a kind of compensation, a memorial that would live on in human memory.

Her husband was born in the Hôtel de Lalande in Bordeaux, and played in its halls during the first five years of his life, when his childhood was still his own. Then the Revolution came, destroying everything. Virginie chose to give him a replica of this lost time, a symbol of hope – proof of a rare kind of love. It brings the great history of the Pichon-Longuevilles to an end.

The final pages in the Pichon-Longueville saga

Two centuries' worth of momentous history ended with Virginie. In her, the story of Joseph and his children, reaching back 120 years in all its thrilling poetry, came to a close. She had decided to leave her estate to one of her husband's nephews, but he died before her. The vineyard was thus left to his widow, also known as the second Comtesse de Lalande – yet another woman. And then, after an unknown time, it was passed on to several Lalande family heirs, who shared control of the estate.

Virginie died in 1882 at the age of 84, just as the dual catastrophe of phylloxera and downy mildew was arriving in the Médoc. She would not live to see the terrible years that followed, and perhaps, for the sake of the story's poetry, this was not such a bad thing.

The Age of Crisis and Disease

In 1882, the vineyard was still enjoying a propitious era. Virginie's heirs, all of them from the Lalande family, might have believed they had come into a goldmine. Despite the powdery mildew crisis, people had become so accustomed to seeing these châteaux yield what had been invested in them that they failed to remember that vines are live plants and therefore fragile, that buyers' tastes evolve, and that weather can pose major problems. The year 1880 marked the beginning of forty years of crisis, during which one of Pichon-Lalande's owners became so frustrated that he wrote a letter asking his estate steward whether Pichon should halt its winegrowing operations altogether.

The Médoc châteaux faced these challenges as best as they could. Unfortunately for the Château Pichon-Lalande, it lacked a leader like the ones it had known in the past. Several different heirs managed the property together. None of them lived at Pichon, or even in the Bordeaux region. An estate steward did what he could to satisfy all parties. Throughout this long and bleak period, a lackluster cast of characters sent orders by letter from Paris, Bayonne, and Perpignan, visiting the château infrequently. The era drew to a close when the château was sold to two young and enterprising men, Louis and Edouard Miailhe.

Disastrous management

Like the rest of Médoc's vineyards, Pichon-Lalande lived through three nightmares at the end of the century: phylloxera, downy mildew, and counterfeiting. The scope of these catastrophes for winegrowers at the time may be compared to the plagues of Egypt. Phylloxera was not, as has been widely held, the most serious: downy mildew and counterfeiting caused greater and more severe devastation.

It would be impossible to examine every detail of the complex relationships between the various Lalande heirs in this short history. Essentially, Virginie's designated heir died before she did, leaving a widow, the second Comtesse de Lalande. She passed along the responsibility to her children, who managed the vineyard from afar. Two of her daughters were married, and so it fell to their husbands to manage the vineyard in their wives' stead. These two men were Armand d'Arthez, a sharp and intelligent dandy as well as an elegant automobile sportsman in Paris, and Joseph de Lacroix, a sour-tempered Catalan squire. They held responsibility jointly with their brother-in-law, the young Comte de Lalande de Bayonne. The Comte, a generous man with limited motivation, was saddled with the hardest tasks, such as dealing with merchants; he loathed this contact with a world that was not his own. Business was conducted in writing, at pre-telephone speeds, and an on-site estate steward named Gabriel Vigneaux kept the books and ran the estate.

Such management would have been inefficient under ordinary circumstances, and it was nothing short of disastrous when compounded by the ruinous scourges that befell the vineyards. It will come as no surprise that merchants took advantage of the situation and of the young count's naiveté: Pichon-Lalande's prices fell to those of *troisièmes crus*, and sometimes dropped even lower. The château itself lay vacant all too often, and nobody had the financial means necessary for its upkeep. And so it remained in the condition in which Virginie had left it, not unlike Sleeping Beauty.

Phylloxera

Phylloxera is a tiny yellow aphid. Its propagation is slow and complicated, and mystified the people of the time. It reached the vineyards of Pauillac around 1880, unintentionally imported with American plants by winegrowers in Languedoc from roughly 1832 to 1840 and in Gironde around 1860. The female aphids feed on the roots of vines, which subsequently die. They then produce winged, sexed offspring that fly off, mate, and lay winter eggs under the bark of other vines. In the spring, the eggs hatch and the insects attack the roots. The cycle begins

Left: the second comtesse de Lalande, also known as *Veuve Carlos* (Dowager Carlos). Already widowed at the time of Virginie's death, she managed the cru for ten to fifteen years before putting her son and her two sons-in-law in charge.

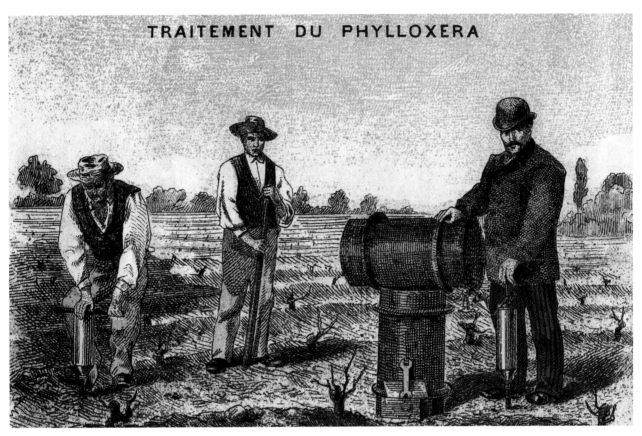

Left: *L'artillerie de la vigne (A Vineyard's Artillery),* 1900 advertisement by Raoul Chauvreau Fils company.

Above: phylloxera treatment with carbon disulfide via injection nozzle. Illustration by A. Merle, c. 1910, for *Les Maladies de la vigne* (Vine Diseases) by V. Vermorel. The technique was not very effective and was replaced by another: a trench was dug around each vine and filled with an insecticide/fertilizer solution. Though the method kept phylloxera at bay for a time, only grafting onto American plants proved a permanent solution.

again, while some of the aphids infiltrate the leaves and form galls.

Contemporary methods failed to eradicate phylloxera. As we now know, the proper solution was to graft French plants onto American ones, which are naturally resistant to the parasite. But it is a little known fact that despite the devastation, Médoc's *grands crus* managed to contain the insect, and delayed vine replacement as long as possible. Grafting onto resistant American plants caught on very slowly and belatedly in Médoc, where growers believed that keeping the heritage of their 200-year-old plants intact would preserve the quality of their wines. A number of contracts and bills of sale, including several from Pichon, state that the wine is "guaranteed to be without American plants." Médoc, which is usually the

first region to adopt new winegrowing innovations, remained extremely cautious in this respect.

The vines were first treated with carbon sulfide, which was injected into the ground with a large syringe known as a *pal* or *gastine*. But while this labor-intensive process more or less contained the insect, it failed to destroy it, and hence the vines grew weaker. Substantial quantities of fertilizer, first natural and then manufactured, were added to improve their resistance.

Treatment with potassium sulfate carbonate was attempted two or three years later. Winegrowers dug troughs around each plant, filled them with insecticide, and poured 30 liters of water to kill and drown the aphids living on the roots, using the potassium as fertilizer.

The use of large amounts of water and fertilizer violated the principles for vine quality that the Médoc had discovered so painstakingly. They specifically recommend giving the least amount of water and fertilizer as possible, thereby encouraging mature vines to seek out food from deep within the earth in order to absorb the mineral flavors of each *terroir*. It was as if a wave of panic had swept the region, causing disregard for the fundamental rules of quality winegrowing.

Pichon-Lalande's register overflows with the estate steward's daily notes, typically after the harvest, specifying how many men were sent "to root out phylloxera." Contrary to a persistent myth, the numbers indicate that phylloxera was relatively contained and did not destroy harvests like powdery mildew. Downy mildew was a different story.

Downy mildew

Downy mildew, a nearly indestructible fungus, also came to France in American plants. It turned up in Pauillac in 1882, sparking a new crisis just two years after phylloxera first appeared there. Anyone who has tended fruit trees knows that insect damage pales in comparison to cryptogamic diseases. The reproduction cycle of these one-celled organisms is infinitely shorter than that of aphids, which is itself extremely brief. Left alone during a rainy year, major cryptogamic diseases can strip an entire apple tree, pear tree, or vine.

Like powdery mildew, downy mildew needs dampness in order to spread. *Peronospora viticola*, a type of mold, penetrates both the plant tissue of the leaves it feeds on and the grape clusters. In healthy vines, the leaves convert sunlight into sugar and feed it to the fruit, which serves as a reproduction vehicle once it has absorbed enough energy. When afflicted with downy mildew, the vine's leaves fall off, and the besieged grapes, which are normally nourished by the leaves, do not ripen properly. Contemporary studies conducted by Alexis Millardet and Ulysse Gayon, professors at the Faculté des Sciences in

Above: an 1886 Pichon-Lalande receipt for carbon disulfide to fight phylloxera.
Below: back-mounted *bouillie bordelaise* mildew spray treatment – highly ineffective in a rainy year. Illustration by A. Merle, c. 1910.

Rosebushes, like sentinels at the ends of the rows, signal aphid attacks.

Below: mildew illustration by A. Merle, 1910. The fungus prevents photosynthesis in the leaves, which provides sugars for the fruits.

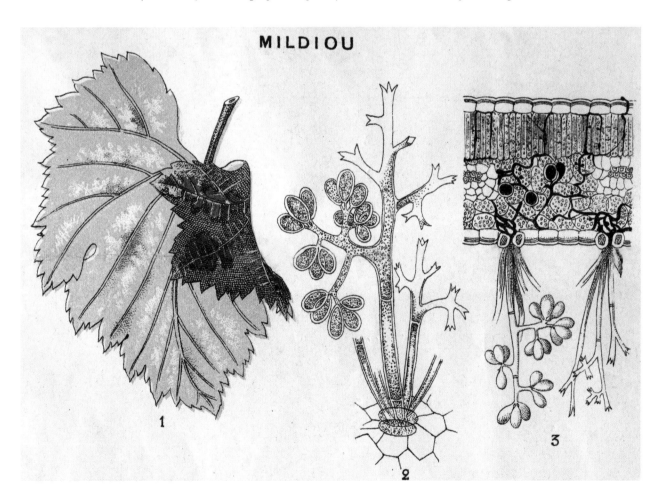

Bordeaux, found that downy mildew can cause a vine to shed up to 90% of its leaves, which turn brown and fall off, meaning the fruit can no longer absorb energy in the form of sugar. During the summer, the microscopic fungus releases spores. These spores grow as soon as they come into contact with water on the leaf surface, leading to rapid spreading. The spores survive the winter, waiting to produce the next generation in the spring.

Through this process, downy mildew altered the very nature of the grape must, and the adjective *mildiousé* – infected with downy mildew – was coined to describe the undrinkable and un-sellable wines of the 1880s. "The loss of sugar content varied from 35% for Cabernet Sauvignon to 77% for Petit Verdot, which is substantial; acidity increased by 17.7% to 37%, depending on the type of vine."*

Confronted with a mightier foe than powdery mildew or

phylloxera, winegrowers were defenseless and willing to try anything. Their approach was less speculative than in the past: this time, the university used its experts and laboratories to devise a solution. While their knowledge was certainly limited compared to today, scientists managed to resolve the problem within six years, an eternity from a winemaking perspective but very quickly given their rudimentary understanding of biology. The answer came with the accidental yet fortunate discovery of a copper sulfate solution, which was sprayed on the vines as a preventive measure. Professor Millardet noticed that vines treated with copper sulfate in order to deter grape thieves before the harvest at Ducru-Beaucaillou had remained healthy. He conducted laboratory tests and confirmed the preventive effect of the mixture, which

* R. Pijassou, *Le Médoc*, p. 765.

became known as *bouillie bordelaise* (Bordeaux mixture). But during wet years, when constant rains washed off the solution faster than the wine workers could apply it from the tanks they carried on their backs, the fungus spread too rapidly to be contained, and the harvest was largely destroyed or *mildiousé*. This was the case in 1910 and 1915, for example, when the *grands crus* were often downgraded and sold as ordinary red wines.

Counterfeits and falling prices

It is clear that the Pichon vineyard was on relatively solid ground by 1888 or thereabouts. Pylloxera and downy mildew had both been contained, if not eradicated. Just when the vines had regained their health, however, counterfeiting and falling prices reared their ugly heads in the Médoc – and it should be mentioned that the châteaux were indirectly and partly responsible for these new crises.

Indeed, they had sold their undrinkable *mildiousé* wines of the 1880s at high prices. Because its *grands crus* still carried the prestige of previous years, the small 1883 harvest, absolutely massacred by phylloxera and downy mildew, sold for 1,4000 francs a barrel at Pichon-Lalande. The notoriously *mildiousé* 1884, 1885, and 1887 vintages sold for 1,600, 1,800, and 2,450 francs a barrel, respectively. The other *grands crus* were not far behind. By selling undrinkable wines at high prices, the major *châteaux* exposed themselves to considerable backlash. Once the situation had improved, their public image was so damaged that a legendary wine like the 1900 vintage sold for a paltry 600 francs at Pichon-Lalande.

Even worse, this practice and the widespread use of sulfur or its chemical derivatives opened the door to counterfeits.

Rumors, confusion, and partial or misconstrued information began to circulate in the press and by word of mouth. The wines were portrayed as "chemical" products, and doctors discouraged people from drinking them, even though sulfur treatments to combat powdery

mildew had originated 40 years earlier. Laboratories tried in vain to prove that the wines only contained minuscule traces of the chemicals, fighting a losing battle against discredit and prejudice.

Counterfeiting was the third nightmare to strike the wine industry. Several types existed. Because wine was now "chemical," counterfeiters and "Bordeaux bootleggers" had free rein. At best, they shamelessly diluted Bordeaux wines to obtain, as the Comte de Lalande described in a letter, "300 barriques from 100."* They labeled ordinary wines Château Lafite or Pichon-Longueville. At worst, they brazenly produced "wines" with water, alcohol, crystallized sugar, and coloring agents, passing them off as a Mouton Rothschild or a Grand Vin de Bordeaux.

Some counterfeiters went so far as to set up stands at major wine expositions, purporting to sell Lafite, Pichon, Cos, and Latour wines at affordable prices – all of them produced miles from Bordeaux in "cellars" in Kalamazoo or Timbuktu. Buyers, who inevitably felt disappointed and deceived, blamed the Médoc châteaux, and journalists accused the estates of being in cahoots with the counterfeiters.

As a result, English consumers and longtime customers supplanted Bordeaux's *grands crus* with whisky or less expensive Bordeaux wines like so-called *crus bourgeois* or even cheaper wines. There was talk of the "victor of the distiller over the vigneron."** Whisky, which until then had been a purely Scottish phenomenon, now entered a golden age.

Consequently, prices plummeted even further. Adding to the dismal situation, the common practice of soaking the bases of vines in a nutrient solution led to excessive yields: from 1900 to 1907, Pichon-Lalande harvested an unprece-

* In the 18th and even in the 19th centuries, Chartrons merchants crafted wines for English consumers by blending Médoc wines with Spanish and Rhône Valley wines. But this traditional practice was sought after by both buyers and consumers, and has nothing in common with what the counterfeiters would later produce.
** Written by Sarah Bradford in a book on port, quoted by R. Pijassou, *Le Médoc*, p. 826.

dented quantity of grapes, twice the normal amount and up to four times that of some years. Enormous yields combined with slow sales and a poor reputation devastated the estates. The beginning of the century was a time of desperation for estate owners, who often ended up throwing in the towel. Despite their laborious efforts, sales barely covered their costs, and failed to do even that some years. Bordeaux wine merchants took advantage of the situation and bought the struggling châteaux.

A constructive reaction

Something had to be done to guarantee each bottle's authenticity to buyers and to burnish the tarnished image of fine wines. The creation of the Union de Crus Classés in 1901 was the first step. The union ensured the origin and traceability of each wine and initiated legal proceedings against counterfeiters. In 1905, Parliament voted in an anti-counterfeiting act driven by members from Bordeaux. Over time, each château would be required to bottle its own harvest onsite, but this only went into effect many years later.

During this dark period, the true visionary – and there was always one in the Médoc – was Nathaniel Johnston, a merchant-proprietor at Ducru-Beaucaillou. Like Comte Duchâtel during the powdery mildew crisis, he was a pioneer in the widespread use of *bouillie bordelaise* and an advocate for protecting labels against counterfeiting. He stands out among the first to assume the presidency of the Union de Crus Classés in Médoc.

But this constructive reaction did not produce results immediately or easily. Prices perked up around 1908, but catastrophic years such as 1910, 1912, and 1913 curtailed this growth.

War and the end of an era

The war brought a new set of disasters. Wine is meant for sharing; it is a complement to friendship, communication, merriment, joy, and vivacity. In the West, its central role in the Bible – from the Song of Solomon to the Last Supper – establishes it as creating bonds between man and man, between man and woman. Wine and war are at odds: markets close in both enemy and ally countries, people have other concerns on their minds, men are called up from the vineyards, diseases are poorly treated, and things are put on hold for better days.

The departure of the estate steward, Gabriel Vigneaux, a hero in such dismal times, and his probable death, is evident in the estate's increasingly neglected register. Nothing is bleaker than war, even in a vineyard where day upon day of work, blue skies, and rain marks the passage of time. The book's pages grew erratic as its keepers lost the will to chronicle the day's events. They recorded less and less: a few bribes here and there, and then nothing at all. The second Comtesse de Lalande died in 1914. The young Comte Charles-Pierre followed her in 1915, and D'Arthez perished in 1916, perhaps on the front. The remaining family members were Mathilde de Lalande, who died in 1923, and her inconspicuous sister, Henriette-Marie, who lived until the sale of the château.

In Perpignan, the bitter Joseph Lacroix, who had always complained about the cost of quality winegrowing, died in 1920. With the exception of Joseph, all of Pichon-Lalande's heirs died childless. He passed on his mentality to his own children, and as a result, none of them was willing to move to Bordeaux and take a chance on a château in such poor shape after 40 difficult years. Its people were gone, but its *grands crus* lived on: the Pichon-Longueville Comtesse de Lalande château was sold, and a group of unforgettable Bordeaux natives took over its management.

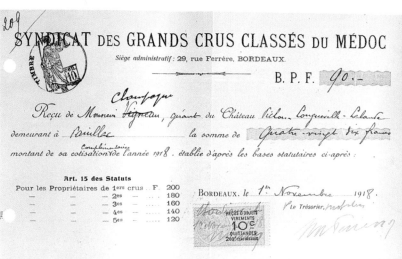

Above: 1907 advertisement for Pichon-Longueville Comtesse de Lalande.
Below: 1918 form attesting Pichon-Lalande's contribution to the Union de Crus Classés, in charge of combating fraudulent wines. Its director's name was Champagne!

THE ERA OF GREAT COURAGE
LOUIS AND EDOUARD MIAILHE

In 1925, with Médoc in shambles, two energetic self-starters took the helm at Pichon-Lalande: Louis and Edouard Miailhe. But the difficulties of the past lingered tenaciously, dashing any possibility of significant improvement. The Miailhe brothers faced not only the challenge of repairing recent damage, but a new string of ordeals. These included the 1929 crisis, the disastrous weather of the 1930s, the Second World War and the occupation of Médoc, the difficult postwar period, and the devastatingly harsh winter of 1956. There were a number of successes, but, unfortunately, the best vintages of the era appeared at the worst times; the brothers could not take full advantage of the 1926-1928-1929 series, which arrived too early, or the 1945-1947 series, which had no real market so soon after the Liberation.

This chapter will be told partly in the voice of Madame de Lencquesaing herself, owner of Pichon-Lalande and daughter of Edouard Miailhe.

The Miailhe family

My grandfather, Frédéric Miailhe, the father of Louis and Edouard, was born in 1867. His mother, Lovely Solberg, belonged to a prominent Norwegian family of brokers that had been in Bordeaux for many years. Frédéric Miailhe looked like a Viking, with a pale complexion, porcelain eyes, and a gentle gaze. He was a talented intellectual in both the physical sciences and in the classics, and won the Latin rhetoric contest at Bordeaux's Jesuit school, Saint-Joseph de Tivoli. But by 1907, this distinguished Latinist had also received a license to drive petroleum-powered cars. He was headed for the École des Chartes when family destiny called him away, and he took over the family's brokerage office, Fouquier et Miailhe, which had been in Bordeaux since the 18th century.

His wife, my grandmother, Adèle Fourcade, belonged to a family from Chalosse, not far from Béarn, with a strong tradition of working the soil. Her mother, Elise de Bourran, came from the Mauritius branch of the Bourrans, which brought an air of the islands to the family. Grandfather and Grandmother Miailhe, the former instilled with the Voltairian spirit of the Enlightenment

Frédéric Miailhe and his wife Adèle, parents of Louis and Edouard. Frédéric, a wine broker and owner of Château Siran, came from a long line of brokers and château owners from the 18th century.

and the latter with the Jesuit rigor of her education by the Ladies of the Assumption in Bordeaux, complemented each other perfectly and had loved each other since childhood. They had three children, including Germaine, the middle child, who died at a young age.

My grandparents owned the Siran château in Labarde, where they stayed for part of the year. I spent some of the best moments of my childhood there with them.

The 1914-1918 war

While they shared a generous streak and a taste for hard labor, Louis and Edouard were otherwise diametrically opposed, both physically and in personality. The 1914-1918 war changed the course of their lives, interrupting their studies and bringing them together.

Louis, the elder brother, an intelligent realist with a strong constitution, was a true man of the soil, close to his employees and passionate about his vineyards. With a Rabelaisian sense of humor and great generosity, he often presided over elaborate meals in his Coufran château, a home of bounty which produced a Médoc *cru bourgeois*.

Educated by the Jesuits, Louis served in the military for three years beginning in 1911, sustaining a tear in his Achilles tendon. He was discharged. But when war was declared in 1914, he decided to continue serving despite his injury, declaring, "Since I can't walk anymore, I'll fly planes instead." He received his license to fly Nieuports and conducted several photographic reconnaissance missions behind enemy lines. Because of his age at the time, he spent seven years serving his country. He appears in photos in his aviator jacket, with his leather helmet peeping out from the cockpit. He adored flying, and became an ace pilot.

Edouard, who was six years younger, suffered from poor health and died prematurely of acute bone cancer in 1959. Tall, elegant, and refined, he meticulously sought perfection in all things and was a deft equestrian throughout his life. A diplomat at heart, he once intended to pursue a career in foreign affairs. Hoping to enter the cavalry, he passed his exams in 1915 and became a non-commissioned officer at the École de Fontainebleau. But because he subscribed to the newspaper *La Croix*, he was demoted to the trenches and given the job of setting up telephone transmissions on the front lines at Verdun. We know, of course, what life was like in the trenches at Verdun. Just barely 18 years old, he wrote to his mother, "I used to be picky, but after this war I'll eat anything!" My grandparents had already lost a daughter and now their sons were in peril, one in planes, which crashed with alarming frequency, and the other on the front lines. They thought they would never see their boys again. "Give up," said my grandfather to his wife. "They'll never come back." But my grandmother prayed endlessly for her children's return, while my grandfather aban-

Left: Louis Miailhe in his pilot's uniform during the war, 1914-1918.
Right: Edouard was assigned to telephone communications in the Verdun trenches.

Above: Edouard, Louis, and their wives.
Below: the two brothers on furlough.

doned his brokerage office and stopped working. What was the point? The plight of his lost sons aside, his vineyards were in a terrible slump. There was little or no wine, and no market for it, as Germany, Belgium, and England were closed to trade. My grandfather buried himself in Greek and Latin literature and philosophy, embracing his passion for history.

The aviator and the cavalier

But in 1918 the two brothers came home unscathed. Their return was hailed as miraculous, and both brothers charged into their next adventure without hesitation. Clearly, the war explains much of their searing intensity, their will to live after so much horror and so many dead companions, but both the aviator and the cavalier had started out with strong characters and tremendous drive, which probably had a lot to do with it as well.

While on leave, Louis had become enchanted by Renée Monvoisin, a young woman he met at the home of his aunt, Isabelle Bompard, in Bordeaux. An orphan, she came from Saint-Quentin in the north and had taken refuge in the south with her grandmother. Immediately upon his return from the war, Louis asked to see her again, but he learned that she had left for the north with her grandmother. "She's the only woman I'll marry!" proclaimed Louis, then 26. He rushed off to Paris and asked for her hand on the Boulevard Malesherbes. The wedding took place in 1919.

Meanwhile, 20-year-old Edouard joined a *rallye* for dance lessons with 11 other young people.* One of the six

* A *rallye* is a group of young people who meet for chaperoned social occasions, including dance lessons, which culminate in a ball; it is similar to the American Cotillion.

young ladies, weary of wordly things, entered a convent, and the group needed a replacement. "I know someone, but she's a bit young," one of the girls offered. Her proposal for a replacement was snapped up, and along came the beautiful Victoria Charlotte Desbarats, who was just 17 years old. Edouard fell under her spell. "I'm going to marry her," he vowed to himself. They were wed on April 4th, 1921.

Renée Monvoisin belonged to the family behind the well-known printing company Maulde et Renou, and Victoria was the daughter of Fernand Odon Desbarats, a former cavalry officer who had married a young woman from London's high society, of the Irish Burke family, who was born in the Philippines. Fernand Desbarats was the friend of Fernand Ginestet, owner of the Château Margaux; he himself later owned the beautiful Château Ducru-Beaucaillou in Saint-Julien.

As the daughter of a cavalier, Victoria rode skillfully, both sidesaddle and astride. Her passion for horses never abated, and she was still riding at 80 years old. My father and mother were an elegant couple both on the town and on horseback. They participated in couples' jumping competitions on the Place des Quinconces in Bordeaux. It is a shame that couples' contests no longer exist. The horses fly over the jumps in unison, carrying men and women in wonderful riding costumes – a magnificent sight to behold. Edouard and Victoria were a truly remarkable team, and won number of trophies on the backs of their horses, Godissar and Chamerock.

It was time to take up a career. Brimming with new ideas, the two brothers took over their father's brokerage office.

The Miailhe brothers' strategy

The Médoc had emerged from the past years battered and torn. People lost faith and began selling their estates. Louis and Edouard took the opposite tactic. Their basic principle was this: if a single château was a bottomless pit from a financial perspective, then several of them managed by the same team ought to be profitable. Their

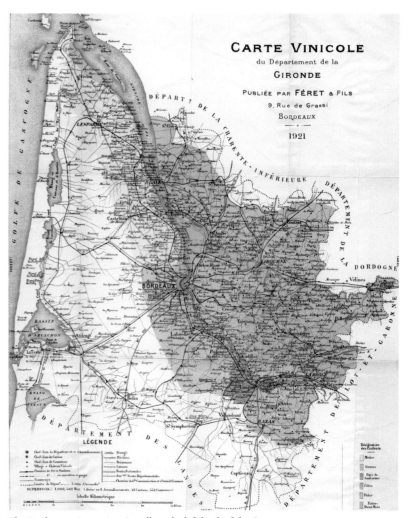

The Bordeaux wine region. In yellow, the left bank of the Garonne, Médoc.

will to live and to believe in a dream, along with their confidence, diligence, and youth, propelled them to undertake this adventure. By developing a number of these châteaux, sooner or later they would make a profit. There would always be a market for the quality wines our region produces so well. Louis and Edouard would rely on their winegrowing experience, derived from their family of brokers and owners, but above all on their labor and strict organization.

Their guess was correct, but Médoc would not reach a prosperous period comparable to the 18th and 19th centuries until the 1980s, after both brothers had died. Thus, they became château buyers, managers of estates owned by others, and brokers. Dealing with suppliers of bottles, corks, tools, and crop protection products, not to mention building companies for ten châteaux, proved infinitely less costly than if they had done the same thing for just one. Without a group of châteaux, it was impossible to stay afloat. Like Pierre Rauzan, they were builders and trailblazers, key players during a period of transition.

They knew their strategy, but to implement it they needed a well-organized office, an energetic team, and money – which they did not have. But, strange as it may seem, money was just around the corner, in the Landes. France was rebuilding itself, and its colonial empire had many needs. Its pine forests produced construction wood, pit timber, crossties, and electricity poles. Pine resin had also become a product of significant value. Landes residents had the means to invest and wanted to diversify their holdings; moreover, Louis and Edouard had a number of friends in the region. Thus, Landes residents greatly contributed to the Médoc's renovation and reconstruction. Crossties financing grands crus – who would have thought of it? It was a perfect example of an integrated regional economy.

Group purchases and management

Louis' wife, my aunt Renée, received war reparations from the Germans for the destruction of her belongings in the north, and with them, Louis bought the Château de Coufran, a *cru bourgeois*, in Saint-Seurin de Cadourne. The brothers went on to buy several other châteaux with the help of their friends in Landes: Pichon-Longueville Comtesse de Lalande, Palmer, Île Margaux, and Citran.

Together, Louis and Edouard managed the following châteaux, ordered from south to north along the river: Siran, their parents' estate in Labarde, *cru bourgeois supérieur*, appellation Margaux; Île Margaux; Palmer, *troisième cru classé*, Margaux, in Cantenac; Citran, *cru bourgeois supérieur*, Haut-Médoc, in Avensan; Ducru-Beaucaillou, *second cru classé*, Saint-Julien, which belonged to Edouard's parents-in-law; Pichon-Longueville Comtesse de Lalande, *second cru classé*, Pauillac; Coufran, *cru bourgeois supérieur*, appellation Haut-Médoc, in Saint-Seurin de Cadourne, north of Saint-Estèphe. They also occupied other functions at La Tour Carnet, *quatrième cru classé en appellation Haut-Médoc*, which later belonged to Monsieur Magne, another Landes resident, and the Château Peyrabon in Saint-Sauveur. Nine châteaux – today, it would constitute a small Médoc empire. With this critical mass, the brothers were able to buy stakes, corks, barriques, and sulfates at the lowest price. It also meant they sold millions of bottles in some years. Even though they ran a successful brokerage office, selling this much wine required close relationships with the Place de Bordeaux market.

Pichon-Longueville Comtesse de Lalande

In 1925, this château was bought by a company founded by Louis and his investor friends in the Landes. It was sold by Henriette-Marie de Lalande and the Lacroix children of Perpignan.

The purchase of the château provided for staggered payments in seven annuities. But within two years of the sale, one of the shareholders declared bankruptcy.

Louis Miailhe asked his brother to participate in this joint venture as a replacement, and Edouard accepted.

From then on, the brothers had full responsibility for managing Pichon-Lalande, with a combined share of 55%. And so my father became part of the history of Pichon-Longueville Comtesse de Lalande, which I inherited in 1978 as part of the Miailhe estate. The company of shareholders endured until 1978 and beyond, depending on the inclinations of its members.

Management, offices

Managing the group of châteaux entailed a great deal of effort, but Louis and Edouard were hard workers endowed with complementary skills. They were interested in everything: economy, finance, history, art history, and wine memorabilia. Their sense of organization was flawless, as were their team spirit and respect for their employees, who, admired them in turn. Driven in business affairs, yet always generous, they were unifiers, always on the lookout for new ideas – a necessity during those difficult times.

A man of the earth, Louis woke every day at five in the morning to tour the vineyards in his Renault, provide on-site management, and make important decisions for various matters; he returned home late each night. While Louis remained loyal to his Renaults, Edouard preferred Hotchkiss cars for their elegance and reliability. Like his brother, Edouard spoke several languages. He spent less time in the vineyards than at the office, negotiating and dealing with companies and foreign customers. Throughout his life he maintained his distinct penchant for building relationships, diplomacy, and travel. From Samarkand, Esfahan, and Sri Lanka, to Guangzhou or Manila, he had endless passion for these hubs of civilization.

The brokerage and management office stood at 42 Cours de la Martinique, at the corner of the Rue de la Pomme d'Or in the heart of the Chartrons neighborhood. It was a

Right: Pichon-Lalande at the home of the Maharajah of Kapurthala.

Victoria and Edouard Miailhe on Chamerock and Godissar. In the background, Ducru-Beaucaillou, property of Victoria's parents.

hive of activity, with a large and loyal secretarial staff in constant motion. The office also managed a wine merchants' group in Rivesaltes that dealt in *vins médecins*, or "booster wines," from Algeria, which in some years were used to improve wines. Relying on their knowledge and information, Louis and Edouard offered what today would be considered consulting services for sales and purchases of Médoc estates. They often served as intermediaries in these types of transactions.

Grandfather Miailhe strolled to the office each morning from 24 Cours de Verdun. He sat down, read, listened, and participated, always wisely and delightedly. In the afternoons, he visited the suburban children's hospital in Bouscat run by nuns from Saint-Vincent de Paul. He managed the hospital on a voluntary basis for 40 years. I sometimes went with him on Thursday afternoons to play with the disabled children staying there, who were referred to as "abnormal" in the language of the time.

As if to encourage the two young winegrowers, the weather was perfect in 1926, 1928, and 1929. This piece of luck helped them emerge from the crisis and confirmed the choices they had made. These vintages went down in history and are nothing short of magical for wine connoisseurs.

1929 crisis and the disastrous 1930s

The following decade, however, was a dreadful time. The weather of the 1930s never allowed the grapes to ripen.

The 1926, 1928, and the legendary 1929 vintages were rated, respectively, 18/20, 19/20, and 20/20. The 1931 vintage, on the other hand, received a 4/20. The year 1932 came away with a pitiable 0/20. The 1934 vintage was the only one to receive a quality score of 17/20, and 1937 came in at an acceptable 14/20. The following years – 1938, 1939, 1940, and 1941 – ranged from 2/20 to 12/20, and were thus impossible to sell.*

The Médoc was in a tragic state. Still, some vintages were improved by Algerian *vins médecins*, and our family's Rivesaltes office did a lot of business. Friendly relationships had been built with these Algerian winegrowers, who developed interest in the Médoc châteaux which had lost value over the years. Edouard and Louis provided consulting services for their purchases, and a wave of Algerian buyers appeared in Médoc. These included the Canafirinas in Belgrave, the Constantinis at the Château Barreyre in Arcins and the Château Brillette in Moulis, which had belonged to the Du Perrier de Larsan family, and others.

The two brothers became prominent figures in the Médoc. Like Pierre Rauzan before them, they mastered every aspect of their craft: working the soil, brokerage, consulting, the enormous quantities of product they were moving, and understanding the far-off customers drinking their wines. Their dynamism made them a force to be reckoned with.

May-Eliane Miailhe, on bicycle, and her sister Monique c. 1931.

The 1939-1945 war

We were at Siran when war was declared. There is a photograph of my grandfather, mother, brother, and sister in front of a wall at Siran that displays a general mobilization order. We understood the seriousness of this development. Born shortly after the armistice of the First World War, we grew up on our parents' and grandparents' stories of the Franco-German war that had lasted more than four years and resulted in so many deaths.

* Figures from the Tastet-Lawton brokerage firm.

Above: Monique and May-Eliane in 1940.

Below: France under the Occupation. German soldiers tasting grapes during the Bordeaux harvest, autumn 1940.

The phony war opened a new and difficult chapter that might go on indefinitely, for all we knew at the time. France, of course, had complete confidence in its Maginot Line.

My father and Grandfather Miailhe were unwavering realists, and always stayed abreast of current events. Together, they decided to protect our family from bombs and rationing, and planned to take in refugees if necessary. We spent the first winter of the war at Siran, just 35 minutes from Bordeaux by train, where we could remain in contact with the office and our newfound pensioners. It was during this time that two of my parents' friends – wine merchants from Trieste – arrived at Siran with their families, explaining that Mussolini's fascist Italian government was persecuting Jews and that they had decided to leave their country temporarily. They asked us to help them find a place in the Médoc until conditions improved.

In addition to being a major Trieste wine merchant, Monsieur Montuori played first violin in the city's orchestra. He and his wife had a young son of five or six named Serge; the other family had a seven-year-old boy and a nine-year-old girl. We gladly offered to set them up in the nearby Château Palmer, an estate we loved and used for business dinners.

The living rooms were fully lined with floral sea green chintz in the style of Napoleon III. The ebony furniture covered in floral fabrics was elegant, comfortable, and welcoming. One of the château's wings extended to the home of the estate steward and his wife, Pierre and Yvonne Chardon, a kindly couple known throughout the Médoc for their talent. Yvonne was a gifted cook who tended the garden beds and created stunning floral arrangements.

And so we moved the two couples and their children into the wing nearest to the Chardons' home. We made constant bicycle trips from Palmer in Cantenac to Siran in Labarde. We were neighbors throughout this first winter of the war, spending many a wonderful evening together at Siran. We played chamber music in Grandmother's drawing room over cups of tea, the fire crackling in the fireplace. My mother played the piano, Monsieur Montuori the violin, and little Serge kept time standing on his footstool. It was my first opportunity to accompany a great violinist on the piano as he played Fauré's "Berceuse."

Grandfather's radio, which we called the wireless, connected us to the outside world. Everything seemed calm this first winter of the phony war, but my father still expected us to work on the vegetable garden each day: who knew what troubles the future held in store? Indeed, our situation took a turn for the worse the following spring, with the debacle of June 1940, the failure of the Maginot Line, the roads crowded with refugees, news of the German troops approaching through Belgium and pouring into northern France, and the arrival of our cousins from Verdun and our friends from Paris. They were to spend the next few years with us at Siran.

The war was shaping up to last longer than expected. Returning to Bordeaux was now out of the question. I was 15 years old in the summer of 1940. We put things in order at Siran, setting up a boys' dormitory in the linen room for the Vautrin cousins: Jacques, age 16; Bernard, 14; and Paul, 8. The historian Colonel Carré and his wife, who were childless but accompanied by their nieces and nephews, first lived at Siran and then at Macau, near Labarde.

My grandfather's predictions were correct. Presided over by Grandfather and Grandmother Miailhe, our dinners overflowed with people. Proper manners were strictly enforced, but the mood was astonishingly cheery given the situation. Our house was packed with children and overseen by Grandmother, a genius in domestic affairs. The colonel and Grandfather, both history and literature buffs, had animated conversations about many fascinating topics. The overall effect was a very pleasant atmosphere. No matter what happened outside, we felt safe.

Candles and oil lamps were still our only light sources. Each child was given one candle a week for his or her candle-holder. But this didn't stop us from gathering around a single flame to play cards, once the others had

been used up. At night, we dressed up as ghosts and lurked about the staircases of the château, dragging heavy chains; the next morning, we would put on innocent faces and ask the colonel or his wife if they had slept well. Pranks aside, we were serious children. In the evenings, we walked the estate park, reciting the rosary, singing devotional songs entreating God to save France. We placed gravel in our shoes to make our walks around the park all the more arduous, and add to our sacrifice. God decided to ignore our prayers: suddenly, the Germans were in Bordeaux.

Maréchal Pétain had moved into a mansion owned by my maternal grandparents, the Desbarats, at 304 Boulevard Wilson. With just 25 kilometers between Bordeaux and Margaux, the Germans were on our doorstep. How could we save our Jewish friends at Palmer? Once again, my father and uncle decided then and there that they had to protect them until a new solution came along.

There was no time to wait. The first German military motorcycles and their sidecars were arriving in the Médoc, and the German authorities immediately requisitioned Château Palmer and, a few days later, the two Pichon-Longueville châteaux, Comtesse, which belonged to us, and Baron, on the other side of the road.

Our friends were in urgent need of our help. In a single night, with the help of Pierre Chardon and a very small number of workers, we built a wall behind the kitchen at Palmer, cutting off the halls leading to our Italian friends' apartment. We then camouflaged it with rusty racks containing old bottles. Behind the wall, the two couples and their children had to remain completely silent until we could devise a plan for their escape.

After the harvests the following October, my father and uncle finally managed to organize their getaway. Armed with false documents and *ausweis*, or identity papers, they drove the families in Uncle Louis's two wood gas-powered Renaults from Labarde to Bayonne, where they hoped to catch the next boat to Argentina. I will never forgot those two cars stealing off into the dark night, setting off on this extremely risky enterprise. As I watched

Edouard and Victoria lunching, about 1937-38, during one of their long rambles on horseback, a favorite pastime.

the lights disappear on that cold, wet October night, I felt sick at heart, doubtful that they would all make it through the many German checkpoints along the way. I truly believed I would never see my father again.

To reach Bayonne, the caravan had to drive through Bordeaux and take highway 10, then the Route des Landes by way of Labouheyre, in the middle of the forest. We knew that inspections by the Germans were frequent and could have devastating consequences. But this time, God heard Grandmother's rosaries (three rosaries of five decades each) and all of the children's fervent prayers. Our Jewish friends safely reached Argentina (we found them again after the war), and Uncle Louis and Edouard returned to Médoc as if nothing had happened.

War had come to France to stay: we were in occupied territory. The demarcation line separating us from the free zone was not far from Bordeaux, slightly to the east, near Langon and Sainte-Foy-la-Grande. Médoc found itself wedged between the free zone east of Bordeaux and the Atlantic Ocean on the west, where the Germans were building coastal fortifications known as the Atlantic wall. The German navy converted Bordeaux's harbor into a major submarine base, using the Bec d'Ambès as its fuel reserve. To the south, the Spanish border was a prohibited zone for French citizens.

Each person was quickly issued ration cards. The Germany army requisitioned all horses, both workhorses and mounts. Watching them go was a wrenching experience. Crop protection products for the vineyards were nowhere to be found, many men were put in prison, women and children were left to work the vines and fields. A group of 250 Germans moved in to Pichon-

Lalande; the officers who requisitioned it had asked us to take out all of the furniture. This is how we managed to save it.

The rooms were completely empty, littered with bales of hay for the soldiers to sleep on. Rifles and machine guns hung on the walls. Rain seeped in through windows left open by the troops. The hay was wet, the floor was rotting away, and the pungent odor of lard, which the young soldiers used to clean their black boots, pervaded the rooms. Their rain-drenched coats smelled of wet wool. They tried to dry off by kindling massive fires in the fireplaces. It is a miracle that Pichon did not burn down during the war.

In the vineyard, cows and oxen did the work of the requisitioned horses. Poor weather devastated the 1941 harvest, and 1942 was not much better.

But what happened to all of the precious old bottles stored in our châteaux? Amazingly, not a single one was stolen. It should be remembered that Germans were great wine connoisseurs and one of Bordeaux's key markets. It should also be remembered that, when the Occupation began, the German army firmly believed it would win the war and thus chose to safeguard these treasures to drink over the years.

Before the war, Bordeaux had developed close ties with merchants in Bremen and Hamburg, represented by the Boemers and Seinitz families, who were also charming old friends of ours. For this reason, the German government appointed Monsieur Boemers and Monsieur Seinitz as *Weinführers*, the former in Bordeaux with a rank of colonel and the latter in Bourgogne. In Champagne, the situation was very different and ended tragically with the arrest, deportation, and death of our friends there.

When our friend Boemers turned up in uniform at my father's office and announced himself as an old friend, he was told that, given the circumstances, friendship was out of the question and we would simply obey his orders as long as he wore the German army uniform. When he was dressed normally and not performing official duties, on the other hand, friendly relations could be resumed.

May-Eliane Miailhe, 1945.
Right: contemporary Austrian glass, engraved and enameled.
Following pages: at left, engraved wedding cups from Germany
and France, early 19th century. Right, antique glasses from various
countries (Czech Republic, France, Italy, etc.), produced using various
techniques. Pichon-Longueville Lalande collection.

All of the estate owners adopted the same position, and each year Monsieur Boemers bought our harvests for the German government at a set price – or an "approved price," as it was called. Our stock of older bottles was respected and sold at normal prices depending on demand. Of course, the English, Belgian, and Danish markets no longer existed, so Germany was the only outlet for Bordeaux wines.

As the war went on, it was unclear how the children could keep up their studies. We continued to send the oldest to Bordeaux to receive their high school diplomas. The children between ages 12 and 16, including myself, took correspondence courses and studied French, Latin, and physics with Grandfather, geography and mathematics with Colonel Carré, and English, Spanish, and piano with my mother.

This is how we spent 1940 and 1941. But as the war raged on, the all-important qualifying exams for the final year in high school loomed on the horizon. We made a partial return to Bordeaux, right when the Americans began bombing the submarine base with greater intensity, especially on nights with full moons, which we usually spent in the basement.

One New Year's morning, as we were on our way to our parents' room to wish them a good year, the ceiling, damaged by a recent bombing, collapsed on top of them. We had trouble finding them under all the debris, amid so much dust and plaster. We lived not far from the banks of the Garonne, and both the German submarine base and the Bec d'Ambès gasoline depot were undergoing increasingly intense bombings. The year I sat for my philosophy diploma, oral exams for history and geography were replaced by written tests, as there were not enough teachers to follow the standard protocol.

After Pearl Harbor, between 1943 and 1944, our American allies' strength heartened the Resistance and gave us hope for a favorable outcome. The German troops grew more nervous and obstinate; food, goods, and clothing were more and more scarce. The line in front of every shop counter was growing. Our shoes had flexible wooden soles. But more and more of the allied planes targeted by German anti-aircraft guns were flying over France.

My father often took me to visit his friend General Brutinel, the former chief commander of the Canadian army in the 1914-1918 war and a native of Gers. This brilliant graduate of the École Polytechnique suffered from severe arthritis and had to use a wheelchair. He lived in the Château de Lascombes. As a Canadian and an invalid, he was off the German Kommandantur's radar and worked for the British Intelligence Service right under the Germans' noses.

We spent many hours with him at Lascombes, where he followed the armies' movements and secretly picked up news from the BBC. We discussed history and political economy; he and my father told stories of Samarkand, Persia, and Mongolia. The general would sometimes ask my father to assist with the escape of a British officer who had parachuted into the occupied zone in Médoc or near Bordeaux, and my father would entrust me with some of these missions, since the Germans were less suspicious of a blonde teenage girl with long braids.

This was our little secret, and not one other person at Sira – neither my mother nor my grandparents – ever knew about it. I have dazzling memories of these evenings at Lascombes, where my father and I would go in our little Rosengart car. I knew that learning from these bright and cultivated intellects and enjoying the warmth of friendship made these moments very special. Because I tended the vegetable garden and fruit trees at Siran, Général Brutinel gave me a book about vegetable gardens written by Vilmorin. He wrote the following dedication: "Planting two seeds where there was only one is to create, and to create is to serve." These words have stayed with me throughout my life.

1945

In 1945, the end of the war coincided with one of the best vintages Médoc has ever produced. The weather could not have been better for winegrowing. Despite the tragic

May-Eliane Miailhe's maternal grandparents.

Above: Fernand Odon Desbarats, cavalry officer and owner of Ducru-Beaucaillou. At left, his wife Mary, née Burke of Ower, from an old Irish family based in the Philippines.

context that enveloped us, this magnificent year was like a gift from God. But there was nobody to buy it, so it sold at the price set during the war. Germany was bankrupt; Holland, Belgium, France, and England were battered; the American market did not yet exist. In Europe, Switzerland was the only option but could not possibly have taken our entire inventory. In this new time of peace, Bordeaux produced a series of great vintages: 1945, 1947, 1949, 1953, and 1955. The wartime prices enforced by Germany were set at 80,000 francs a cask and did not begin rising until the early 1950s.

Edouard Miailhe and his daughter May-Eliane wearing a *terno*, a traditional Filipino dress, 1952.

The brothers go their separate ways

Following the long and gloomy war, it took many years to rebuild our economy. The border with Spain closed in 1936 and was still closed in 1948, the year I was married. That year, people still needed ration cards and tickets to obtain bread, meat, butter, dairy products, soap, and sugar. Above all, the postwar period brought a number of huge changes in the professional lives of Louis and Edouard Miailhe. Both brothers were called upon to take over the management of their wives' estates.

For Louis, this was the printing giant Maulde and Renou on Rue de Rivoli in Paris, as well as his wife's affairs in Saint-Quentin in Oise.

For Edouard, this was rebuilding his wife's extensive real estate holdings in Manila, which were decimated by the Japanese occupation and American bombing campaigns. The situation was incredibly complex, involving damages paid by the United States for Spanish and English property belonging to French heirs. To make matters worse, the title deeds had disappeared in all the chaos and the administration in the Philippines was extremely disorganized and slow. Our Irish uncle William Burke, a professor at Santo Thomas University, was dead; my grandmother, his sister, was too old and lived in France. There was nobody onsite to look after our property and oversee its reconstruction.

My father quickly gathered that all the confusion over the estate, restoring our buildings, and the endless steps for settling war damage and succession issues in a country under American mandate would require him to spend more and more time in the Far East.

With their new family obligations, the two Miailhe brothers decided to restructure and divide their business in 1953, putting an end to 30 years of cooperation and partitioning their vineyards.

Louis kept Coufran, already his own property, to which he had added the Château de Verdignan in Saint-Seurin de Cadourne. His share also included the Château Citran, the family's villa in Saint-Jean-de-Luz, the Miailhe Frères brokerage house in the cours de la Martinique, in Bordeaux and the Rivesaltes office. Edouard received the family property of Siran, home to their mother Madame Frédéric Miailhe; Île Margaux; their interest in Château Palmer; and a majority share in Pichon-Longueville Comtesse de Lalande; and the forests in the Landes. He took charge of managing these vineyards.

This process was difficult and painful for both brothers, but it was a crucial step. The future demonstrated the wisdom of organizing the estate into separate branches: barely six months later, Edouard died of cancer at a relatively young age on December 3, 1959, and Louis's beloved Renée passed away six months later, in January 1960.

After losing both his brother and his wife in such a short time, Louis decided to retire. Until his death in 1982, he spent the colder half of the year exploring Greece, Turkey, Sicily, Italy, and Spain. Naturally, he always brought a full caravan with him: friends, family, children, nieces and nephews, and other guests – including his old chaplains who had reached retirement age. He learned everything there was to know about Napoleon's campaigns, visiting and studying the sites of each battle. He was never without an entourage, and never stopped presiding over his famously sumptuous dinners. At the age of 80, he still enjoyed camping in the mountains of Europe and rising early to attend the mass given to us by one of his priests, including his first cousin and our uncle, Don Joseph de Vatheire.

And so ends the story of the Miailhe brothers, who managed the Château Pichon-Longueville Comtesse de Lalande, among other estates, and passed it along to the next generation. The brothers were each endearing in their own distinct ways. Toward the end of his life, Uncle Louis recalled how his younger brother always opened the door for him and moved aside to let him go first. Based on exemplary courage, work, and elegance, their education was a gift from their parents and accounts for the magnificent adventure they shared from 1920 to 1953. They were visionaries and builders, always realistic, clear-headed, and active. Together, they crafted ways to emerge from the misfortunes that befell our Médoc. Like Pierre Rauzan in the 17th century, they never saw the extraordinary growth that would follow, but like him, too, they never stopped forging ahead.

Madame May-Eliane de Lencquesaing

As for the Château Pichon-Lalande, it was to some extent shielded from these difficult times. Grouped together under the aegis of the Miailhes along with vineyards such as Palmer, Ducru-Beaucaillou, Siran, and Coufran,

Pichon-Lalande was able to avoid disaster during this transition period. The wine was well-made and the vineyard was properly managed, but Pichon's fine wines could not blossom and develop a unique personality until they flew solo. This would be the legacy of Edouard Miailhe's daughter and her husband, Hervé de Lencquesaing, who took over the vineyard in 1978. But first, the succession question had to be resolved, a process that took many years.

The succession of Edouard Miailhe

As with Virginie's heirs, the Lacroix and Lalande families, we will not go into the details of this complex, lengthy, and difficult succession, which involved Edouard Miailhe's heirs and, indirectly, Pichon-Lalande's minority shareholders. Managed by Alain Miailhe and then by an interim administrator, Pichon-Lalande had many great successes for 18 years, but its destiny remained up in the air. In July 1978, the heirs drew lots to apportion the estate's various components. Fate chose May-Eliane de Lencquesaing, Edouard's youngest daughter, to shape the future of Pichon-Longueville Comtesse de Lalande.

A New Dimension
May-Eliane and Hervé
de Lencquesaing

We are now entering an era in which history and the present coalesce, making firm conclusions difficult. Nevertheless, considering its progression over the past 27 years, it is safe to say that Pichon-Lalande entered a new dimension. After May-Eliane and General Hervé de Lencquesaing took it over in 1978, the Château Pichon-Longueville Comtesse de Lalande enjoyed a number of opportunities that led to unprecedented success, never before seen in its history.

Of course, all of Bordeaux's vineyards, large and small, benefited from a series of very fine vintages from 1978 onward. Other outside factors came into play, including the revolutionary advent of enology, which could improve more modest years and triple production in better years. Moreover, the world developed a renewed passion for fine wines after so many sluggish years. But these circumstances fail to account for everything.

In a time when many *grands crus* were falling into the hands of financial holding groups which were slowly crowding out individuals, Madame de Lencquesaing and her husband played a decisive role.

May-Eliane de Lencquesaing

The author, having known May-Eliane de Lencquesaing well and having worked with her, would first like to underscore her incredible energy. She tirelessly pursues her goals, no matter how many times she has to change her approach. She devotes herself fully to this pursuit, using common sense to tackle matters that seem complicated from the outset by setting the right priorities. She has the tenacity and drive needed to create a lasting mark. But this alone would not be enough. May-Eliane's actions and deliberations reveal her complex and powerful personality. She is open to the most sophisticated philosophical questions yet wields a practical sense that keeps her eye fixed on the fine points and challenges of the people with whom she interacts. Her generosity of spirit and heart is a key part of her character. No matter where she is, this devoted Christian strives to aid the weak and the poor. In 1962, she transformed her Paris apartment into a refugee camp for French settlers repatriated after Algerian independence. In the United States, she gave English classes at Fort Leavenworth for foreign officers' families. As an elected member of the local government in the Pas-de-Calais, she persistently cultivated community, organization, and new ideas, and supervised day camps for 25 years.

May-Eliane has not rested since she arrived at Pichon-Lalande. Elected Grand Chancelier of the Académie du Vin de Bordeaux, she immersed herself in cultural projects, traveling to China to help create Bordeaux's first *commanderie* in Shanghai and to lay the foundations for a sommelier institute. She never hesitates to offer a sympathetic ear or to empathize with others, no matter how humble or significant. The epitome of a lifelong learner, she regularly signs up for classes, particularly when life leads her in a direction that requires new skills, eagerly opening books and taking notes in order to expand her knowledge. She is deeply interested in all sorts of fields and topics, from Egyptology to Italian Renaissance art, from wine to social matters, from the 1789 Revolution to her collection of glass objects and sculpture in *pâte de verre* – the only one of its kind in France. She is passionate about history, dedicated to seeking perfection, and prone to the type of self-reflection that leads to sensible action.

Along with all this, May-Eliane exudes imagination, joy, and humor, laughing uproaroariously and contagiously while recounting a comical memory. Nobody is perfect, of course: underneath her many qualities, she has her shortcomings like everyone else – which we will sagely avoid mentioning. Her story will give a more thorough picture of her character, but it should already be obvious that such a leader was a great asset to Pichon-Lalande. As the decline of the Lacroix and Lalande families demonstrates, wine is first and foremost the men and women behind each barrel and vine.

Moreover, May-Eliane de Lencquesaing made the important decision to live in the château, which had not been done since Joseph de Pichon-Longueville during the Revolution. Pichon's management became more attuned to human and material realities.

A winegrowing château is not just a business. It is a family residence where people are received as friends, a lived-in home rather than an anonymous museum or a staged "lifestyle" exhibit that reaches out its empty arms to nobody but fleeting guests. Pichon-Lalande casts the magical spell of an ancient family, with Sophie's paintings and portraits of Virginie and Joseph adorning its walls. Each nook and cranny has its own history, from the library to the coat rack strung with the leash belonging to Piccolo, a King Charles spaniel who must be walked every evening in all sorts of weather – all to the surprise and delight of visitors.

We once again turn to Madame de Lencquesaing for a firsthand account: "In 1978, Pichon-Lalande was like a sleeping beauty. Since Virginie's death, nobody had made it their everyday home – and for good reason. Its furniture, layout, facilities, and modern conveniences had remained unchanged or had changed very little; there was a tree growing in the scullery!" It took time to renovate the Comtesse, but the restoration was designed to respect its history and spirit.

The château's fine wines are just as lively as the château, brimming with the velvety texture and power that make many of Pichon-Lalande's vintages irresistible. With a noble variety of Merlot and part of its land in Saint-Julien, this unique and, as many tasters have noted, "feminine" Pauillac bears the stamp of the woman who made it what it is today, first along with her husband and, from 1990 onward, with a team she handpicked.

Interior views of the Pichon-Longueville Lalande château.

As for the general, he was also – as his son Edouard de Lencquesaing tells us in the book he dedicated to him – a bulldozer.*

General Lencquesaing's career

Born in 1920 in the Château de Loppem in Belgium, Hervé de Lencquesaing belonged to an old family from Flanders that had long served the king of Spain (one of them, Michel de Lencquesaing, was even an officer in the Philippines). They swore allegiance to the king of France when Louis XIV conquered the region in the 17th century.

Laprée, the family's château, was located near Saint-Omer, nestled in an enchanted park accented with the languid curves of an ornamental pond. The contours of this reflecting pool and of the paths that wind through trees with straight, towering trunks, along with the delicate blue of the northern sky, inspire a dreamy, calm, and peaceful mood. When the cool air begins to caresses your shoulders, you go indoors and catch a glimpse of a bygone era through the window of a salon adorned with Italian-style landscapes. You can almost hear the notes of a romantic *lied* song or see a water fairy roused by the fog.

Hervé de Lencquesaing would always cherish his visits to Laprée, with its décor reminiscent of Alain-Fournier's classic tale of adolescence, *Le Grand Meaulnes*, between two battles raging far away. After an exceptional education, he began pursuing an army career just as war was approaching and Hitler was gaining ground through calculated provocations. The young Henry began a prepara-

* Edouard-François de Lencquesaing, *Général Hervé de Lencquesaing, L'héroïsme discret d'une époque*, Paris, Éditions du Félin, 2003. The notes that follow are drawn from this fascinating work, which sheds light on many little-known facts. Along with remarkable analyses and portraits of the era, the book features excerpts from the officer's campaign notes as well as from the diary he kept as a young man, which lend it the authenticity of a primary source. Hervé de Lencquesaing's testimony also provides an invaluable historical account of the second armored division and the beginning of the Indochina war.

Hervé de Lencquesaing and Victoria Miailhe on horseback in Saint-Jean-de-Luz c. 1950.

tory program for Saint-Cyr in Versailles, where he struggled with the elite school's strict requirements and his own difficulties, arising from his diverse interests. "I'm obsessed with everything," he lamented in his diary, in which he regularly questioned himself and the world around him in order to grow. Having too many interests, he realized, would for a long time be an obstacle rather than an advantage. While some made sacrifices, he would not. "Become brilliant in everything and never be mediocre!" was his command to himself. In high school, he received a science diploma and then, three months later, a philosophy diploma.

War was declared and his father was drafted while Hervé finished his studies and successfully passed Saint-Cyr's entry exam during the Battle of France in May 1940. The debacle took place, his father was taken prisoner, and the roads flooded with crowds of refugees fleeing combat zones and the German troops. Appalled by this catastrophe, Hervé returned to Laprée and then drove with his

mother and young brothers to Deauville, Pomerol, and then on to Cannes, where they took refuge. As the family's wait stretched on, the Vichy regime was established and the Germans moved into Laprée. In December, Hervé was finally admitted and entered the École de Saint-Cyr, which had moved to Aix-en-Provence in the free zone.

The official position was made explicit to the officers in training: the goal was to prepare for retaliation against the German enemy. Military training was conducted with this in mind, drawing on the lessons in modern war so clearly elucidated by de Gaulle in the years before hostilities began. There was instruction in guerilla techniques to be used one day against the Germans.

Hervé chose to join the cavalry and completed Saint-Cyr with a rank of second lieutenant in August 1942, as American forces won a decisive battle against the Japanese at Midway, the German forces had been stopped at Moscow and Leningrad, and the Battle of

Above: at left, Hervé de Lencquesaing at age 20. At right, in the tower of Sélestat, in Alsace, in combat in 1944.
Right: marriage of Captain de Lencquesaing and May-Eliane Miailhe, July 16, 1948, in Saint-Jean-de-Luz.

Stalingrad was about to begin. He was required to attend cavalry enforcement school in Tarbes but only spent a few weeks there. When American forces arrived in North Africa, the Germans responded by invading the free zone, taking over the school as they went. Hervé and his friends, who were poised to defend themselves with weapons, were asked to submit to the enemy, who had posted machine guns around the school. The young people felt profoundly deceived: rather than a vehicle for retaliation, the Vichy regime was nothing but a smoke-screen. "It's over," wrote Hervé in his diary. "Poor soldiers whose fearful leaders think them unable to fight back. An armistice army, a peacekeeping army, lining up and marching... Is that all we're good for?"

Hervé and his friends refused to give up. They decided to go to liberated North Africa, where the French army was

regrouping. After several weeks spent making the necessary contacts, he found the right network and in February 1943 secretly crossed the Spanish border in the Basque Country. In his bag, he carried only the necessities, which sum him up well: a knife, warm clothes, sugar, a chessboard, money, and Montaigne's *Essays*. In Spain, Hervé and his companions witnessed the Spaniards' support for the Americans and their relative neutrality. Indeed, the tide was turning. The Germans' defeat at Stalingrad foreshadowed what was to follow, and Franco closed his eyes to these activities. Hervé reached Casablanca in May 1943.

After much incident, he joined the armored division led by his uncle, General Leclerc, an enormous and highly modern military machine that was gathering and preparing in the Témara forest between Casablanca and Rabat.

Hervé became the officer of a squad of howitzers mounted on tank platforms. He then joined the second armored division. He traveled to Hull, participated in the Normandy landings, injured his Achilles tendon while fighting in harsh clashes outside Alençon on August 12, and missed the liberation of Paris. Hailed as an "elite officer" by his superiors, he reclaimed his post on August 26 after fleeing a military hospital and contributed to the campaign to liberate Alsace under freezing conditions. During these long and sleepless nights, he battled bitter temperatures and extreme fatigue on the snowy peaks of the Vosges; on watch, he read Céline's *Journey to the End of the Night*. Hervé continued into Alsace, where, following the liberation of Strasbourg, he treated his men to a dinner served by German women on a tablecloth made from the enormous Nazi flag that flew over the city. Another skirmish in Strasbourg landed him in the hospital. After a short mission to shrink the Royan pocket, where the Germans had entrenched themselves by closing access to Bordeaux's harbor – yet another episode in Germany's crushing defeat – Hervé crossed the Rhine, rode to Schondorf on horseback, and helped liberate Berchtesgaden, where Hitler's retreat, the Eagle's Nest, was located. On May 25, he received orders to return to France.

Having lost many close friends in his class, Hervé felt out of place among civilians. He could not relate to their infatuation with success and their careers, their carrying on as if the war had been but a brief accident they had already forgotten. He volunteered to join a number of his army companions serving in the second armored division in Indochina. But the war had taken a new direction there: rather than a war of liberation, it was now a revolutionary war without any rules, waged against an invisible enemy set on defending its pursuit of freedom – according to its own interpretation of the term. Hervé was unprepared for this type of conflict, in which politics play at least as great a role as classic military factors. He quickly grasped the difficult situation, his uneasy position, and the insufficient means at his disposal. He heroically defended the civilians under his supervision

during the communist Viet Minh's horrendous night-time insurrection in Hanoi, and was seriously wounded yet again in late December of 1946. On his hospital bed, Hervé was awarded the Légion d'Honneur by General Leclerc, and was sent home to France.

Just barely recovered, he was put in touch with Edouard Miailhe about an assignment in the Philippines. In Edouard's daughter he recognized the woman he had always dreamed of, and the two were married in Saint-Jean-de-Luz in July 1948.

Each stage of Hervé's active career was rooted in the Cold War and decolonization: staff training in Lille; on assignment at the Command and General Staff College in Fort Leavenworth, near Kansas City; as commanding officer of the 501st tank regiment in Rambouillet; and Algeria, where instead of the combat zone he was assigned to staff headquarters in the Sahara and then in Constantine. The crowning achievement in every officer's career is the time he spends commanding a prestigious regiment. Hervé de Lencquesaing was given command of the 18th dragoon regiment in Raims-Mourmelon, where he went to live with his wife and four children. There, he was promoted to the rank of officer of the Légion d'Honneur. After a brief stay in Besançon, Colonel de Lencquesaing was twice assigned to a post in the United States as a liaison officer instructor at Fort Leavenworth's training facility. After two years at the helm of CLEEM, the French military's center for foreign languages and studies in Paris, he finally decided to retire. General Hervé de Lencquesaing had lost his idealism during the Algerian War, never understanding why France abandoned this tortured country without making more of an effort to protect its communities, and trying to help develop a solution similar to Nelson Mandela's in South Africa.

Moving to Pichon-Lalande was a new beginning for him; he gave all of his energy and enthusiasm to this most recent and unexpected adventure.

He and May-Eliane had four children: Edouard-François in 1949, Hughes in 1950, Violaine in 1955, and Anne Catherine in 1959.

Pichon was fortunate to gain such strong leaders. Their

military background, ability to adapt to the trickiest environments, and daring industriousness no matter what the challenge were crucial factors in the vineyard's renaissance and its future successes.

We once again turn to May-Eliane de Lencquesaing for an overview of the vineyard's evolution.

Coming to Pichon-Lalande

"While living in the Pas-de-Calais, I was extremely busy with the local government, of which I was an elected member. I led a number of groups, including a senior citizens' club I had created, and of course, the day camps; I had more activities than I could count within the district. Taking over Pichon-Lalande did not thrill me and would require complicated reshuffling. My husband, General Hervé de Lencquesaing, had been in retirement since 1974. He had always loved Pichon and been extremely fond of my father. To him, this new opportunity was very exciting; learning the art of making wine, a product of the earth and of human labor, appealed to the soldier in him, and to his agrarian roots. Moreover, the peregrinations imposed by husband's military career had kept me away from Bordeaux for 30 years. I didn't know anyone there anymore and was a much more hesitant than he was to take on this challenge, but I quickly decided to meet it head-on.

So we found ourselves living at Pichon-Lalande a large part of the year. The château hadn't undergone any sort of modernization since the time of Virginie. Having been used as a summer home, it didn't even have any heating. With its finances in such a sorry state, asking the minority shareholders to get involved to install heating was out of the question. No matter! Military men are used to adapting, and living in a freezing house during the winter was no obstacle. We set up an electric radiator in one room, and our only secretary, Madame Bergez, ate her meals with us at a bridge table in the corner. Everyone kept their coats on.

I remember our very first dinner party. My husband and I sat at the bridge table with my uncle, Louis Miailhe, and Monsieur André Cazes, owner of Lynch-Bages and mayor of Pauillac. Uncle Louis and André Cazes told stories of the past. It was a very joyful occasion.

The first vintages

1978 brought us luck. Things had not boded well at first, with a late, staggered, and irregular flowering period, cold temperatures in May and June, and rain for the first half of July. But on July 16, our luck changed, and fate chose us to take up the torch once again. A heat wave suddenly appeared and continued until the end of the month. As the saying goes, August determines the quality of the grape must, and August was magnificent that year, followed by a very warm September. And so we began some of our latest harvests ever, on October 9th for Merlot and on October 19th for Cabernet Sauvignon. This Indian summer, which was often so lovely in Médoc, gave us a top-notch vintage with a smooth, rich, full, powerful bouquet and Pichon's characteristic finesse.

The late English wine legend Harry Waugh, who was an Honorary Master of Wine and one of Château Latour's directors, wrote about the 1978 Pichon vintage's "dark color, sumptuous bouquet, and great balance." Serena Sutcliffe gave it a 19.5 out of 20, describing it as "a first-class wine of incredible beauty with lace-like length, which could easily be a Lafite."

Regrettably, the harvest was meager at just 36 hectoliters per hectare, not enough to drastically improve our finances.

Many other high-quality Pichon vintages followed the spectacular 1978. The very next year, 1979, also began with a cold and rainy March, but then a run of good weather and light drizzle ushered our grapes into a lush and magnificent maturity. When we began harvesting on October 3rd, Médoc was enjoying another beautiful Indian summer. The abundant harvest went on for three weeks, yielding no less than 350 casks. I soon realized we

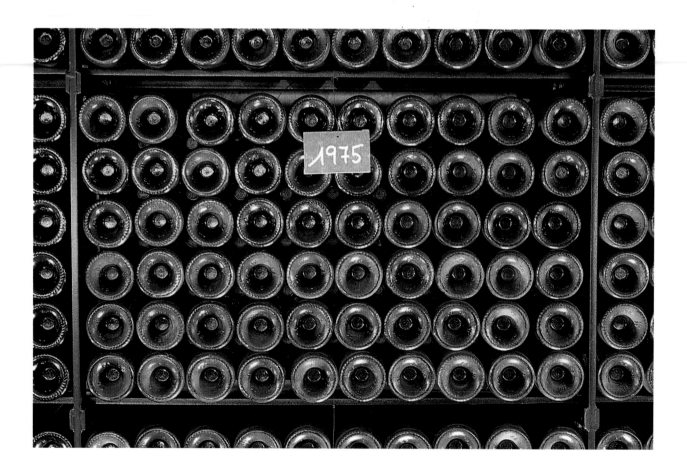

didn't have enough tanks. To avoid diminishing the wine's quality, we had to speed up the pumping-over, extract at a slightly higher temperature, and work around the clock with three teams in the cellar. The managers barely slept; vigilance was the key to making the most of this copious harvest while maintaining quality. We were extremely tired and anxious. I knew that major investments were in order.

We needed stainless steel tanks with spray cooling (coil cooling did not yet exist). I approached the Guérin company, known for its reliability and cutting-edge techniques. It was our first big investment. The 1978 and 1979 vintages would often be compared in vertical tastings for their excellence in very different styles.

Training

In the 1950s and 1960s, the professors Jean Ribéreau-Gayon and Émile Peynaud began developing a new science called enology, which advanced our scientific understanding of winegrowing and winemaking by leaps and bounds. Vineyards around the world began taking steps to modernize. In 1978, I noticed that contemporary techniques bore little resemblance to what I remembered from the 1930s and 1940s, when the wine profession was still reeling from a series of crises and diseases. Enormous progress had been made, and I was aware of my ignorance.

Professor Émile Peynaud, who was Pichon's consultant, encouraged us to take enology classes. Gaining the basic knowledge necessary for understanding tasting and the winemaking process seemed absolutely vital to me. And so we began attending courses at the University of Enology in Talence. The General returned to school with great enthusiasm. We left Pichon-Lalande at 6:30 or earlier in the mornings.

My husband and I were drawn to Émile Peynaud immediately. He closely followed Pichon until the day he retired. He supervised the blending of the 1978 and 1979 vintages, as well as the remarkable and delicate 1981, the

Pichon-Lalande's stainless steel vat room.
Left: old vintages, known as "*de la Comtesse*", in the cave. (see p. 172)

high-quality and plentiful 1982, and the venerable 1983, a typical fine Pauillac with all of its elegance and complexity. He continued to lend his expertise, year after year.

It is important to keep in mind that the administrator assigned to the vineyard in 1971 at the request of Pichon-Lalande's minority shareholders did not have any wine-growing qualifications. Thus, in 1975, I asked my friend Michel Delon – who would later manage his family's estate, Léoville Las Cases – to take over all technical aspects of winegrowing and winemaking, under the administrator's authority. He was responsible for the magnificent 1975 30-year vintage, which dazzles with its power, elegance, complexity, and youth. He successfully retained the fruit and smoothness of this vintage, which is now often characterized by its dry notes. He also supervised the blending of the 1976, a low-yield vintage due to little rainfall that year with notes of spice, anthocyanins, polyphenols, and extreme concentration.

I subscribed to *Decanter* and the *Revue des Vins de France*, immersing myself in works by the professors Peynaud and Pijassou, the professor Guimberteau's notes, and books by Michael Broadbent, David Peppercorn, and Hugh Johnson (*The New Great Vintage Wine Book*). I created my own English glossary for all of the technical tasting terms and began drawing up files on the weather conditions for each vintage from 1900 onward. I then reached out to every journalist with a tasting column at the time.

As I worked, I was flooded with memories of my university studies and my winegrowing roots. I realized that my childhood visits to all of the vineyards and châteaux in Médoc alongside my father and uncle had helped prepare me for my new life. With me in tow, they would speak with the estate stewards, the viticultural managers, whom we called *hommes d'affaires*, and the cellar masters. I unwittingly received a valuable education on a daily basis. Like Thérèse de Rauzan before me, I was heiress to a hallowed ancestral tradition. But I also knew that the classes I took at the Institut d'Études Politiques after my marriage in 1954 and 1955 and my education at the École du Louvre would provide a new perspective on

Pichon's needs. This proved to be the case for the graceful transformation of the park's buildings; Palladio and studying the Brenta villas served me well.

The wine world

As we had in the past sold our wines exclusively through an importer in each country, I wanted to return to trading through the Bordeaux marketplace, so I made the rounds of all of the brokers' and merchants' firms, sharing my decision to sell my wines in the traditional manner. Taking an unconventional approach, I visited brokers and merchants at their places of business, gaining insight into each one.

Next, I had to learn about the complex relationships between the various wine organizations: the Union des Grands Crus (UGC), the Bordeaux Interprofessional Wine Council (CIVB), the Syndicat des Crus Classés, the Syndicat d'Appellations, the Bordeaux Wine Academy, and the Commanderie du Bontemps. Returning to Bordeaux after 30 years, I didn't know a soul and felt bewildered by all of these professional groups and associations. I asked my good friend Philippe Guyonnet-Dupérat to guide me through this maze, and he coached me with infinite patience and kindness. The army had taught me about strength through unity, so I was fully prepared to join these organizations and work as a team. Philippe Guyonnet-Dupérat was director of both the Union des Grands Crus (whose president was Pierre Tari, owner of the Château Giscours) and the Bordeaux Wine Academy (whose Grand Chancelier was Monsieur de Fonrocque-Mercier). Another friend, Jacques Hébrard, offered his assistance and welcomed me into the Bordeaux Wine Academy.

The business world

In 1978, Jean-Jacques Godin was the estate steward of Pichon. He was an intelligent man and an expert in the

trade, and the vineyard was very well-maintained. Unfortunately, we eventually had to part ways. He was very hard on the staff, and I soon noticed that relations between the two parties were strained. The comings and goings of the vineyard and cellar employees were a constant puzzle. As a result, and despite Jean-Jacques Godin's opposition, I immediately reestablished a number of customs that brought me closer to our staff and renewed their confidence in the management: steak dinners after the draining process in November and pruning in March, and a *gerbaude* party at the end of each harvest.

Shortly after my arrival, I wanted to set up a Christmas tree for all of the mothers and children under 12, complete with Santa Claus and gifts – an unprecedented practice in the Médoc. This entailed several epic telephone calls to owners who were a bit taken aback by this initiative. The tree eventually went up in early January, so we used it to celebrate the Feast of the Kings with dancing around the nativity scene. It gave me the chance to get to know the mothers and to help establish friendly ties within our company.

I later began recognizing our longtime employees with bronze, silver, and vermeil medals for long service, and soon after added a pre-Christmas gala dinner, inviting both our employees and their spouses. These yearly dinners, sometimes based on a theme chosen by the staff, now include roughly 130 people. I often use the occasion to present medals and certificates.

As part of a five-year investment plan, we created new accommodations for the staff, building a group of houses in the pleasant La Couronne area. Housing was in great demand, and we were happy to foster loyalty among Pichon-Longueville Lalande's employees.

I soon noticed that the bottling and wine casing workshops located inside the property were causing enormous problems for trucks picking up deliveries. This was my first investment and loan. With the shareholders' approval, we built a workshop and a storage building with a 1,000-square meter floor surface on the grounds of the old vegetable garden. We went on to invest in stainless steel tanks.

Eventually, I was able to buy back the minority shares in Pichon-Lalande held by the shareholders in Landes, who had taken part in our vineyard's development since 1925. They wanted to either sort out their estates or part ways for other reasons. I bought back the shares in several phases, and became Pichon-Lalande's sole owner.

Travel

In 1981, we began going on publicity tours and meeting with collectors, a behind-the-scenes facet of the business which the general public rarely glimpses. Special measures were necessary to regain our wines' erstwhile prominence, to make them known, and to foster a worldwide trend in our favor.

Due to the success of the 1978 and 1979 vintages, I was able to breathe new life into Pichon-Longueville Comtesse de Lalande by presenting it to foreign tasters and collectors. In 1980, my husband and I traveled to England, Switzerland, Germany, and Belgium. The following year, we went to Japan to open the market in the Far East; that year marked the beginning of market globalization, with the United States at the center.

In 1973, the châteaux of Bordeaux came together to form a new association designed to help them tackle the international market. The Union des Grands Crus de Bordeaux included the châteaux of the right bank (Pomerol and Saint-Émilion) and the left bank (the Médocs) – all red wines – and those of southern Bordeaux (the Graves) – red and white wines. Over the years, Pierre Tari (Château Giscours), Bruno Prats (Château Cos d'Estournel), Peter Sichel (Château Angludet et Château Palmer), Antony Perrin (Château Carbonnieux), and Alain Raynaud (Château Quinault) have served as president. Until early 1996, its director was Philippe Guyonnet-Dupérant; Patrick Maroteaux (Château Branaire-Ducru) is its current president.

As part of a UGC delegation, we began touring the United States in November 1981. Its other members included Pierre Tari, Bruno Prats, Peter Sichel, Denise

Lurton (representing the estates owned by her father, André Lurton), and Sophie Schÿler (representing Château Kirwan for her father). In each city we visited, we hosted a tasting and lunch for the media, a big tasting for importers and distributors, and a gala dinner, which was often organized by the Maître de la Commanderie* du Médoc et des Graves.

The pace of these tours was grueling: New York on November 6th; Boston on the 9th; Washington, D.C., on the 11th; Philadelphia on the 13th; Atlanta on the 16th; back to New York on the 18th; Kansas City on the 19th. We used any spare time we had between events to visit importers or to give our own interviews. We received a warm welcome everywhere we went, and the UGC expertly arranged each and every detail (renting the rooms, planning and ordering menus that complimented the wines, serving the wines at the perfect temperature, ensuring professional service, staying on schedule, and maintaining lists of contacts).

We also had to oversee the choice of vintages for the tastings and dinners, send the bottles far enough in advance to allow them time to settle, anticipate theft (a rather frequent mishap), plan our trips so as to meet with as many people as possible, bring thank-you gifts, avoid losing things, avoid forgetting things, shake countless hands, exchange business cards and organize them back in the hotel room, and so much more.

These UGC trips were excellent training for me, whether I was with a small group, as in the 1980s or a large group of up to 50 members for European markets like London, Brussels, Zurich, and Merano. Today, the UGC makes presentations in Asia, North America, Russia, and other locations around the world. Close ties have developed between members representing the various appellations, and an enhanced knowledge of the wines has been attained. Each member of the delegation stands for hours at long tables, pouring wine and

---

* *Commanderies* bring together major connoisseurs and fans of our wines. Connected to the Grand Conseil des Vins de Bordeaux, they serve as important ambassadors for us.

Hervé and May-Eliane de Lencquesaing at a Los Angeles tasting organized by Bipin Desai in 1987.

answering questions; each one presents the same vintage. These remarkable publicity tours are organized down to the last detail. Jean-Marc Guiraud, the director of the UGC for nearly ten years now, does excellent work with the help of his team.

The collectors

My husband and I had just taken the helm at Pichon when, much to our surprise and wonder, we learned about major wine collectors in the United States and Far East. This phenomenon had taken shape after the Second World War. The Americans who had liberated France stayed behind after the war to defend Western Europe against the Soviet Union, discovering Europe's *art de vivre*, its distinct lifestyle, and the joys of fine food and wine in organizations like SHAPE. Enamoured of our country and passionate about our wines, these Americans – doctors, lawyers, university professors, financiers – began putting together extraordinary wine collections after returning to the United States.

These collectors have maintained high professional standards in both their work and their hobbies: Americans like Louis Skinner, Larry Stone, and Stephen Kaplan; Chinese collectors in Singapore like Dr. N. K. Yong and his wife; and in Hong Kong like Maître de la Commanderie Vincent Cheung and his wife, or Agustin Que and his wife. Year after year, they have built collections brimming with the finest vintages and the best crus, each amassing 5,000, 10,000, or 15,000 bottles.

Naturally, they feature cases of all of Bordeaux's *premiers crus*, its foremost *seconds crus*, and other wines that strike each collector's fancy, as well as oversized bottles – magnums, double magnums, *impériales*, and jeroboams. Some collectors have sought out the finest Burgundy wines with equal enthusiasm.

Most often, these collectors belong to clubs like the Chaîne des Rôtisseurs or the Bacchus Society, which welcomed me as a member. At the same time, the Grand Conseil de Bordeaux was setting up *commanderies* in each American city. The collectors became our ambassadors and close friends – in New York, Washington, Philadelphia, Chicago, Houston, San Francisco, Los Angeles, San Diego, Hong Kong, Singapore, and, soon after, Tokyo, Osaka, and Fukuoka.

They are as knowledgeable as they are generous. Through them, we realized that wine, in addition to being a mythical drink, is a herald of our culture and friendship. As Gabriel Delaunay, Bordeaux's former prefect, once wrote, "There is a civilization in wine, that of men who seek know each other, so as not to fight each other." And, according to Shakespeare, "Good company, good wine, good welcome, can make good people."

These collectors offered up their finest bottles – and, often, their oversized ones – to charities and auctions, usually to support disabled children, cancer research, or the fight against genetic illnesses. We became fast friends with these exceptional individuals, and I am delighted to pay them tribute here.

The experience of living in the United States for several years had granted my husband and me a deep understanding of the richness and energy of Americans – their enthusiasm, their intelligence, their seriousness, their professionalism, and their generosity. They should not be overlooked in the history of Bordeaux wines: they drove our wines' spectacular return to the spotlight all around the world, after our vineyards endured so many difficult years.

During these years, we also formed relationships with foreign universities, which shape not only young minds but tastes as well. The British universities of Oxford

Various older vintages served at the 1987 Los Angeles tasting.

and Cambridge regularly buy our wines and have established wonderful collections over the centuries. They found enology clubs and often invite vineyard owners to present their wines and share their knowledge. For that reason, we make frequent trips there, as well as to Leuven in Belgium; I also make presentations at Duke University, Cornell, and Harvard. In France, we are thrilled that clubs have finally appeared at Sciences Po, HEC, ESSEC, ENA, and the École de Management de Lyon. These clubs were created by interested, curious, and passionate students, and I salute them!

Tastings to remember

In the United States, Hong Kong, Singapore, and Taiwan, it often happens that collector friends invite us to conduct a two- or three- day series of events, generally a benefit gala, a grand tasting (also a paying event), and, finally, an auction. The participants' generosity is always extraordinary, as they never fail to offer the very best vintages: a case of 1986 Petrus, a Lafite-Rothschild Imperial, magnums and double magnums of Margaux, Haut-Brion, Cheval Blanc, Mouton Rothschild... The lots are always disputed in good fun, and auctions take place in a friendly atmosphere. Packages often include trips for two or four to our châteaux, naturally with an exceptional dinner accompanied by our finest vintages.

I recall fondly the long vertical tastings of Pichons where I would present twelve, even fourteen vintages in American cities such as Denver, Nashville, and Naples.

One of the memorable friendly tastings I attended was hosted by Dr. Louis Skinner in Miami's Coral Gables, on February 1st and 2nd, 1986. It was a horizontal tasting for the 25th anniversary of the great Bordeaux châteaux' 1961 vintages.

The first session began at 10 am. One wine every three minutes, totaling eighteen wines, were tasted in the first session! Pavie, Bel Air, Clos Fourtet, La Gaffelière, Magdeleine, Figeac, Cheval Blanc, Clos L'Église, L'Évangile, Vieux Château Certan, Gazin, Latour Pomerol, Trotenoy, Petrus, Domaine de Chevalier, Pape Clément, La Mission Haut-Brion...

The wines were discussed and the first session ended at noon. Figeac, Cheval Blanc, Magdeleine, Petrus, Haut-Brion, and La Gaffelière were the winners, "still young for their twenty-five years, complex, virile, elegant..."

The second session was at 2 pm. The following Saint Juliens and Margaux were presented: Lagrange, Saint Pierre, Langoa Barton, Branaire Ducru, Beychevelle, Gruaud Larose, Léoville Poyferré, Léoville Barton, Léoville Las Cases, Ducru-Beaucaillou, Cantemerle, Rauzan-Ségla, Giscours, Malescot Saint-Exupéry, Boyd-Cantenac, Brane-Cantenac, Palmer, and Margaux.

3:30: discussion and conclusion of the second session. Gruaud-Larose, Léoville Las Cases, Palmer and Brane-Cantenac all received quite favorable mentions.

The Saint-Estèphe and Pauillac session began at 10 am on Sunday, February 2nd. Phélan Ségur, Lafon-Rochet, Calon-Ségur, Cos d'Estournel, Montrose, Batailley, Haut-Batailley, Mouton Baron Philippe, Pichon-Longueville Baron, Pichon-Longueville comtesse de Lalande, Mouton Rothschild, Latour, and Lafite Rothschild were tasted.

Mouton Rothschild and Lafite Rothschild were the winners, followed by Saint-Estèphe wines Calon-Ségur, Cos d'Estournel and Montrose, all quite mellow and still young. Noteworthy Pauillacs included Lynch-Bages, Pichon-Longueville Baron (prominent notes of fruit, complex, intense, virile) and Pichon-Longueville comtesse de Lalande (mellow tannins, powerful, distinctive, and... feminine!).

For the 25th anniversary of this vintage, Dr. Skinner presented twenty-five châteaux from his personal collection or provided by friends such as Dr. Marvin Overton, Lloyd Flatt, Bernard Rhodes and Tawfiq Khoury. The gathering brought together thirty-six producers, collectors, journalists and professionals who made up quite an assembly of the wine world's internationally recognized personalities. Such society required the utmost professionalism in the wine preparation, temperature control, glass control, serving, etc.

Our host had chosen an "inner circle" of his old acquaintances to share in all elements of the tasting. As such a tasting is truly a celebration, each meal, even the informal welcome, was designed around a theme, leading up to the final, extravagant banquet. We were treated as distinguished guests by the distinguished gentleman who hosted us.

The next year, 1987, Bipin Desai, University of California physics professor and Bordeaux connoisseur and collector, organized in Beverly Hills (Los Angeles) a grand Pichon-Lalande vertical tasting with wines from 1875 to 1986.

My dear friend Harry Waugh, a charming and vivacious man legendary in the wine world, was master of ceremonies.

The tasting saw fifty-six guests, fourty-four vintages, and four vintages of the Réserve de la Comtesse, the other Pichon-Lalande wine.

The pre-phylloxera, pre-mildew years were represented by the 1875 vintage; those after, by the 1892, 1893, 1899 and the great vintage of 1900. They were followed by the 1917, 1918, 1920, 1921, 1924, 1926, 1928 and 1929. For

the 1930s, the 1934 and the 1937. Next, the 1942, 1943, 1945, 1947 and 1949; the 1950, 1952, 1953, 1955, 1957, 1958, 1959; the 1961, 1962, 1964, 1966, and 1967; the 1970, 1975, 1976, 1978, and 1979; and finally, the 1980, 1981, 1982, 1983, 1984, 1985, and 1986.

All the great vintages, then, were represented, along with some slightly less legendary ones, for the sake of curiosity. Some of them were quite pleasantly surprising.

For the Pichon 1959, the year of my father's death which was marked by a very hot summer, I noted: "a vintage of high quality, the attack is powerful, the tannins round and very present, smooth, with an excellent length, and so young!"

The 1953 magnum had a nose of underbrush and Corinth grapes. It was immense, with superb tannins, and long, very long. Louis and Edouard Mialihe separated in this year.

The 1945, that miraculous, grand vintage at the end of the war years, was very concentrated.

1917: notes of tea, coffee, and spices; light and charming.

The 1900 magnum received a 19/20. As our friends said, it had a "sweet, long finish" and one could sense the difficulty the Lalandes and Lacroix had parting with this abundant and successful wine, made so in part by manager Gabriel Vigneaux.

The 1893 double magnum is remarkable, a 20/20, with dark color and an extraordinary brilliance at once, a round attack, with hints of chocolate and vanilla, and an excellent length. This was the legendary year that the harvest began on August 17th in 46°C (115°F) temperatures!

The 1875 has a very dark color, a powerful nose reminiscent of port, and an excellent roundness on the palate. It was an important vintage in Pichon-Longueville history, produced under Virginie's direction and brought together for the first time with Gabrielle's wine.

Such tastings can be very moving. They pour the results of our ancestors' work into our cups, onto our palate, imbue our conversation with it. They reproduce the climatic conditions that our predecessors had to face, when facilities were not what they are today, when understanding the mysteries of wine was more experiential than scientific – enology had not yet been born.

We greatly admire our American friends' enthusiastic interest in these emblems of our past, and it is thanks to these friends that French wines gained world renown which soon passed on to Asian collectors, in the 1960s, '70s, and '80s.

Other tastings punctuated the 1990s, such as that of Stephen Kaplan in Chicago on April 16 and 17, 1994. A horizontal tasting-luncheon of 57 1959 wines brought these wines together with the expertise of *grand chef* Charlie Trotter. The tasting included wines from Alsace, Pomerol, Saint-Emilion, Saint-Julien, Pauillac, Saint-Estèphe, Sauternes, the Rhône, and the Loire. Stephen Kaplan went as far as to specify from which seller each wine came.

We must mention, of course, the vertical Pichon-Lalande tasting at the Rubicon in San Francisco on the 24th and 25th of February, 1996, given by Georges Sape in conjunction with Larry Stone!

Larry Stone, master sommelier, was aided by Daniel Johnnes, sommelier of Montrachet restaurant in New York at the time, and chef Tracy Des Jardins, a remarkably gifted young woman. The wines were chosen particularly towards the aim of accentuating their scale of intensity. Only the great 1893 was presented separately, at the end, with a selection of carefully chosen cheeses. The wines were presented in the following order, rated out of 100.

First round: 1926 (92/100); 1952 in magnum; 1967; 1980.

Second round : 1928 (91/100); 1953 (94/100); 1957 (86/100) and 1964 in magnum (94/100).

Finally: 1959 (98/100); 1970 in magnum (91/100); 1975 (89/100) and 1985 (93/100).

The 1945 vintage received a 99/100; the 1982, 100/100; and the 1893, whose premature 46° degree harvest we have discussed, was called one of the greatest and most exceptional old vintages, close to the 1899 Lafite and as memorable as the 1847 Yquem.

The bicentennial
of the American constitution

The strong ties developed over the years between Bordeaux producers and our American friends was cemented on September 17, 1987, with the bicentennial celebrations for the American constitution.

Denise Lurton-Moullé and I were invited to present Clos Fourtet, La Louvière, Pape Clément, Giscours, and Pichon-Lalande wines at festivities in Washington, Boston and Philadelphia. I presented the 1979 Pichon-Lalande at a gala dinner in Philadelphia, presided over by President Ronald Reagan. The 1975 and 1970 vintages were served at the French Embassy in Washington.

Quite an homage to our country, when one considers the scope of American production in California. Among American wines, only a 1985 Robert Mondavi Fumé blanc was selected to accompany the Chesapeake crab and scallops.

The death
of General de Lencquesaing

The year 1990 began in Penang, in Malaysia, at the home of our friends Mac and Ann Saw. It ended in November with the death of my husband, carried off by a difficult illness, the first symptoms of which appeared during our stay in the Saws' coffee and rubber plantations.

I stayed with him in Paris throughout his illness, missing the harvest. When I returned to Pichon at the beginning of that November, I set about the blending the 1990 vintage. I knew that the General's passing had left me in a fragile, and perhaps even vulnerable state.

Wary of making solitary decisions, I decided to reorganize Pichon's management structure. I built a management team that surrounded me with young and experienced people. Pichon has been working with this team for 15 years now.

For the estate's technical management, I called on a young agricultural engineer from ENESAD (the Dijon National Graduate School of Agronomy), Thomas Dô-Chi-Nam, who has filled his role as technical director with excellence. For marketing, and then as general manager, I felt it was essential to find someone with enough experience that he or she could take on a certain number of my business trips to give me more time at the estate. I talked it over with my children, and we quickly agreed on my nephew, Gildas d'Olonne, who worked with the International Distillers and Vintners at the Château Loudenne. He had been educated in the vein of British financial adviser Martin Bamford, boasted experience from British business culture, and spoke both German and English. He lived in the Médoc, and his mother hailed from Bordeaux. Finally, I called on Jean-Claude Lafrance to act as financial manager; with extensive banking experience, he was the former director of the Caisse d'Épargne, holding a degree in business from the HEC School of Management in Paris and another in modern literature.

From that time forward, rather than making solo decisions, I discussed each one with my team.

The vineyard's features
and investments

Pichon-Lalande's vineyard stretches to the south of Pauillac, with one fifth located in the neighboring appellation of Saint-Julien. They run along the Château Latour, near the Gironde estuary.

They cover 85 hectares (210 acres), and are planted with 45% Cabernet Sauvignon, 35% Merlot, 12% Cabernet Franc, and 8% Petit Verdot.

We have never stopped investing and growing our activities, both in Médoc and abroad. Among our accomplishments:

• The installation of eight 254-hectolitre (6700-gallon) stainless steel tanks in 1981

• The 1983 extension of the first underground cellar, creating a magnificent 100-meter (330-foot) long terrace overlooking the Château Latour vineyards, with a unique panoramic view of the Saint-Julien and southern Pauillac vineyards, with their 20-kilometer (12.4-mile) estuary, all the way out to the Citadelle de Blaye and the islands. The nearby river explains the quality of the terroir, with its harsh hilly terrain and well-drained soil, and its microclimate, located as it is between two bodies of water, the ocean and the estuary. It is said that great wines should "look at the river," and it is certainly the case here.

• The only way to house the 1,300 second-year barrels, which before had been stored in various scattered buildings, was to build a second underground cellar. In 1986, we hired the Mazières, a father and son architectural team that had built a similar great cellar at Château Margaux. With basket handle vaults and 33 columns, it creates a cloister-like atmosphere, with a calm, almost religious ambiance perfectly fitting for aging wines.

Renovating the château

The Comtesse's château was waiting for the moment of its awakening. It had remained nearly uninhabited since Virginie de Lalande's death. Between periods of disease, crises, wars, and difficult postwar periods, there had never been any opportunity to properly renovate the château in a manner that both respected tradition and brought it into the modern era. It sat waiting to be restored, since storing and aging wine had always taken priority over housing the owners.

Finally, something was done about it – with utter respect, of course, for the original décor chosen by the Comtesse de Lalande. The furniture had been hidden away in the attics to save it during the Occupation. Now it was given a second youth. Above all, this allowed the charm and unity of style found in the Restoration-era furnishings to be preserved.

The immense terrace created by the two partially underground cellars required a redesign of a section of the park that resembles the Palladian gardens in Italy, evoking the gardens in the Brenta Valley near Venice. Balustrades, stone motifs, statues, terra cotta, cypress,

Pichon-Longueville comtesse de Lalande escutcheon with the charges of the Raymond de Lalandes on the left and those of the Pichon-Longuevilles on the right, surmounted by the crown of a marquis, the Lalande family title.

and rose gardens blend into the landscape of boxwood, sculpted sweet bay, Greek oaks, and strawberry trees that the Comtesse de Lalande had created.

Purchase of the Château Bernadotte in 1997

My father and uncle had always been guided by the principle of diversification, aiming to present as broad a range of products as possible and ensuring that they complement one another and take advantage of each other's prestige. This allowed the two men to lower management costs and, in difficult financial situations, to sacrifice a product within the range.

Owning a *cru bourgeois* vineyard located in a quality *terroir* was an interesting prospect: it would enable us to offer the markets and our clients a respectable wine at a lower price. Many wine lovers cannot afford to buy a luxury product like a Médoc *deuxième cru classé* every day of the week. After several years of research, we had the opportunity to purchase the Château Fournas Bernadotte in 1997. This *cru bourgeois* is located near Pauillac, just three kilometers (half a mile) from Pichon in the Saint-Sauveur municipality. Its vines are close to Pontet-Canet and Grand-Puy-Lacoste. The previous owner, Monsieur Kurt Eklund, was from Sweden. For 25 years, he had given his all to bring about the renaissance of this vineyard. The estate was founded in the 17th century by the Bernadotte family, which now sits on the Swedish throne.

Château Bernadotte's wines, which are famed for their consistent quality, are therefore well-known in the Swedish royal court, and the Swedish market has been a loyal customer.

Significant investments have been made since 1997, including the creation of an extremely well-equipped cellar and a second aging cellar, both of them fit for a *grand cru classé*. The château has been entirely redecorated, and Bernadotte is now open year-round to receive Pichon's many friends, who visit regularly. The estate

Above: the South African Glennelly Estate vineyard, in Simonsberg. Right: the traditional *capedeutch* house at Glennelly.

covers 35 hectares (86 acres), planted in 50% Cabernet Sauvignon, 44% Merlot, 2% Petit Verdot, and 4% Cabernet Franc.

Pichon-Lalande crosses the sea to Glenelly Estate

For years, I had wanted our Pichon team, with all its knowledge and experience, to take on the challenge of adapting to a new *terroir* and a new climate, creating a great wine overseas. But where? After several attempts in the United States, which unfortunately did not work out, I looked to other winegrowing regions, such as Australia and Chile.

In 1989, the Union des Grands Crus organized a research trip to South Africa. In fact, many winegrowing estates in the Cape Town area had been planted with our own varietals by French Huguenots in 1688, following the revocation of the Edict of Nantes. It is interesting to note that the great winegrowing estates of the Médoc were also just starting to be planted at that time. At the beginning of the 17th century, Henri IV brought Dutch workers over to drain the Médoc "polders." Such signs from the past have always had an effect on me.

South Africa, which was just emerging from the apartheid years, captivated my husband and me with its beauty, its climate, and the kindness of a well-organized population like the Afrikaners, descendants of the Dutch – and of course with the quality and potential of its wines. But the thought of investing there was the furthest thing from my mind.

Later, I was invited to take part in some important tastings as a jury member, and I started getting to know the estates and wines of South Africa, forming ties of friendship with some of the wine producers.

When I was in London in 1993 as the president of the IWSC (International Wine and Spirit Competition), I created a trophy for the best wine in the world made from at least three varietals. Several consecutive times, following blind tastings by a jury of professionals, the trophy was awarded to a South African wine. The prize, in addition to a cup created by a major artist like Jean-Paul Van Lith or the master Bordeaux goldsmith Rolland Daraspe, was a stay at Pichon-Lalande.

I decided to invite seven of my grandchildren (everyone over 12) on a journey to South Africa, with a safari in the northern part of the country, on the Zimbabwe border, and then on to the Cape Town wineries, with tours and tastings morning and evening. The trip was a wonderful one for grandmother and grandchildren alike – our Afrikaner friends welcomed us warmly.

In 2003, after a number of trips, I was shown a magnificent 125-hectacre (310-acre) property, the Glenelly Estate. It was located on the edge of Stellenbosch, in the heart of South Africa's finest wine country. It borders the renowned Rustenberg estate that belongs to our friends, the Barlows. The estate stretches along the slopes of the Simonsberg mountain, reaching an altitude of 400 meters (1,300 feet).

Located at 35° latitude south of the equator (Pauillac is 45° to the north), Stellenbosch is close to the Atlantic, and enjoys an ocean climate similar to the Médoc's, but also to Tuscany's, with higher temperatures and strong winds. Both the *terroir* and the climate made this an excellent choice for red wines with a blend of Cabernet Sauvignon, Merlot, Syrah, and Petit Verdot.

We have already planted 55 hectares (136 acres), and are looking forward to planting six hectares (15 acres) of Chardonnay and a hectare (2.47 acres) of Riesling to round out our white wine selection. Finally, we will be planting a small olive grove of between two and five hectares (between five and twelve acres), as South African olive oil is marvelously exquisite.

The estate comprises two lovely homes. One of them is of modern design, located on the elevated part of the cirque, and enjoys a gorgeous panoramic view of mountains, valleys, and the ocean off in the distance. The other house is in the traditional *capedeutch* style, with a thatched roof, Flemish gabling, and dark wood flooring. It sits at the

center of a set of gardens, one planted with white flowers, one a rockery planted with different tropical species, and the last a beautiful rose garden with fountains fit for a Persian garden.

The construction of the winery was done by three architects: Frédéric Luscher, from Swizerland, who designed the Dominus winery in the United States; our Bordeaux architect Serge Lansalot; and, finally, the South African architect Tim Zielh.

To me, Glenelly Estate is a very potent symbol. In addition to the high-quality wine estate we have sought to create, it is a nod to the memory of my ancestors, who, in the Philippines, would outfit their boats to set off for London, and always stopped over in Cape Town to load supplies of fresh meat, green vegetables, and wine. In 1855, Grandfather Butler, accompanied by his wife and daughter, my great-grandmother, stopped in Cape Town on their way to London.

There is another important aspect of my investment in South Africa, which can be placed in the context of relations between the northern and southern hemispheres. The best way to help developing countries in Africa is to prove we believe in them, to provide work for them, to help them from the inside.

South Africa has undeniably been making indisputable progress since the end of apartheid. Its laws are strict but sensible; work and investment are both encouraged; respect for nature is a priority; and laws regarding manual labor are going in the right direction.

Many people ask me, "Aren't you afraid? Aren't you taking too much of a risk?" To them I reply that there are risks everywhere, and that I am proud to meet this challenge. It is my way of helping the African continent, and I am not alone in my confidence in this beautiful country and its people.

The Bordeaux Wine Academy

In 1992, following the death of my husband, my friend Jacques Hébrard (Château Cheval Blanc) very kindly invited me to join the Bordeaux Wine Academy. I was thrilled to add a cultural dimension to the Pichon-Lalande wine estate, and to look at wine from more than just an economic standpoint. The Academy brings together different players in the wine industry, teaching and perpetuating the spirit of Bordeaux wines throughout the world – a way of expressing our elegant, refined, traditional culture and *art de vivre*. Beyond its wines, Bordeaux as a city has given the world its share of free spirits, whether during the Renaissance, like Montaigne, or the age of Enlightenment, like Montesquieu.

I never would have dreamed that the Grand Chancelier Alexandre de Lur Saluces would ask me to succeed him. But on June 11th, 2004, he did just that, passing me the torch on the occasion of the Academy's general meeting at the Château Pape Clément.

With this distinction, Pichon-Longueville Comtesse de Lalande regained the recognition and the brilliant reputation it had enjoyed under Baron Joseph and his two daughters, Sophie and Virginie. This new position would allow me to accomplish more than my work as a wine producer, following in the footsteps of Alexandre de Lur Saluces and developing the Academy's cultural message.

National Academy of Sciences, Humanities, and Arts of Bordeaux

In June 2005, I had the surprise of learning from its president, Jean Tavernier, that I had been elected to the Académie Nationale des Sciences, Belles Lettres et Arts de Bordeaux (National Academy of Sciences, Humanities, and Arts of Bordeaux). What had I done to deserve this honor? What would my new responsibilities be? I was overwhelmed. My first thought was one of gratitude to my father and my four grandparents, to whom I owed so much, and who would have been so pleased by the news. I was elected to the seat of Michel Quancart, and was to give the oration praising this remarkable man. My ascension date was set for February 16th, 2006.

History of a collection

Are we born collectors, be it of stamps, postcards, engravings, paintings, or 18th century furniture? I believe we are. To collect is to create ties with certain objects, with their creation, their history, their rareness. It means uncovering their mysteries a bit more every day. In Bath, England, I became fascinated by a charming 18th century glass with a braided stem. The antiques dealer's interest was contagious, and the English glass was the first of many, collected over many encounters with other antique dealers and collectors. Wine and glass make such a lovely pair.

Next came 17th century glasses from France, glasses from Charles X, from the Restoration, antique Murano glasses, Römer glasses from Germany. And, of course, enchanting Bohemian glass in blue, ruby, and gold. The collection now includes Roman glasses, rare glasses from Afghanistan, and even Chinese glasses from the Han dynasty (206 B.C.E. – 220 C.E.).

There are a great number of French glasses in the collection, including some rare 18th century pieces, an interesting assortment of Restoration-era goblets, and a Fabergé ewer from Moscow at the end of the 19th century. More recent times are represented by Gallé, Baccarat, Lalique, and Schneider, and a remarkable piece designed by Cocteau for Daum.

Long ago, glass served as a container – carafes, bottles, ewers, vases, wine glasses, champagne cups. But during the Art Nouveau period, artists like Lalique and Daum used glass as a material to be sculpted, molded, and manipulated. Today, glass sculptures are generally large-scale works, and are relatively little known in France. This in spite of such great French artists as Étienne and Antoine Leperlier, Jean-Paul Van Lith, Jean-Claude Novarro, and Raymond Martinez, who easily rival the Czech schools represented by Jaromir Rybak and Ales Vacisek; Hiroshi Yamano from Japan; the Americans William Carlson, James Watkins, Steven Weinberg, and Marin Rossol; and, of course, the great contemporary master Dale Chihuly. This not to mention the Italian

Le Totem, Van Lith glass sculpture.

school, which includes Lino Tagliapietra and Lucio Bubacco, and the Swedish schools of Orrefors and Kosta Boda.

Glass is magic, born of sand, fire, and human breath. It is humble, like grapes – that wild vine that humans have for centuries transformed into a divine beverage.

In 1994 I met master glassmaker Jean-Paul Van Lith, and Pichon's modern art department was born.

I like the idea that the fragility of glass is a constant in my life.

Spiritual testament

I am still working at over 80 years old – nothing has kept me from it. Health permitting, why not continue giving one's energy, experience, and creativity to our world? I was born in the beautiful month of May, so why not keep this eternal springtime in my heart? You are only as old as you are at heart.

When introducing myself to my illustrious future colleagues at Bordeaux's National Academy of Sciences, Humanities, and Arts of Bordeaux, I told them something I will repeat here: An old vine doesn't give much, but what it gives is the very best of itself. Thus, as an octogenarian, I stand before you with empty hands.

To stop is to no longer make progress. Should I stop? Should I stop making progress? Do I have the right to do so?

We have crossed the threshold into the third millennium, and it is time to inscribe the present in the future. For more than 300 years, the Pichon-Longueville estate has given birth, year after year, to a new vintage – and a new promise.

This link between our land and the people who work it is an expression of our culture and our traditions, and it is a humanist one.

As we have seen throughout these pages, just two families watched over the birth and development of this family estate. They left their permanent mark, making the vineyard what it is today, inscribing the past in its present.

Now, as I preside over its fate with the same love showered upon it by Thérèse de Rauzan, Baron Joseph de Pichon-Longueville, the Comtesse de Lalande, or Edouard Miailhe, with the same attachment to its very soil, passed on to me by my father, my only question is, "What happens next?"

I wish Pichon-Lalande a future that allows it to adapt to the economic circumstances imposed on it by this new millennium, in this world where so many values have been thrown into question.

Pichon is a business. A business does not belong to those who manage it. It is a whole, and it belongs to the people who make it. It may be passed on, and this must be done with an eye to the certitude that it can go ever further, that it can continue to grow. It is up to us to cement the alliances that will allow it to ascend even higher.

May Pichon always be a symbol of quality, and of tradition. May Pichon keep its face and its soul. These are my wishes.

As for the vines, they must be given time, and presence, and heart.

A wine estate is not a wine industry, as modern parlance would have it. Every vintage is different, while an industry entails a product that is always the same, always regular.

A winemaker gazes upon his vines as one gazes at a loved one.

Now that I am past 80, should I retire? There may be some who think so. But how can I leave my vines? Should you ever leave what you love?

Perhaps... if it is for its own good..."

On December 28, 2006, it became a *fait accompli*: the Rouzaud family, of Louis Roederer champagnes, with its own rich heritage, takes up this hallowed family tradition.

CONCLUSION

The story of Pichon-Longueville Comtesse de Lalande does not end in 2007. Directly or by marriage, the same family governed it from 1685-1688 to 1925. That year, the Miailhe family took the reins: Louis and Edouard, his son Alain, and his daughter, May-Eliane. Frédéric Rouzaud of the Rouzaud family, from the Roederer champagne group, succeeded them in 2007. Two families in three centuries: a rare constancy. It allowed us to write this history almost as one would a novel: patriarchs, brotherhoods and their eternal rivalries or absolute alliances, a great merchant, magistrates, politicians, military men, an artist, *courtiers*, barons, countesses, so many remarkable women, such passion, such frailty.

Each generation gave itself unstintingly to this great wine. Would it have been the same had it been overseen by technicians – even the most advanced? There is a dramatic, romantic magic to long family lines, with all their light and shadow, as with the Lur Saluces of Château Yquem. A story like Louis d'Estournel's, who created a great *cru* in the space of a single lifetime, is unique.

The saga of the Pichon-Longuevilles is no less than the saga of French history; it is the history of Médoc vineyards. From the intuitions of its founders to the sumptuous feasts of the Restoration and the Second Empire, from crises to world renown, this is the eventful life story of Bordeaux wine. The characters peopling it are united by this book's true protagonist: the wine of Pichon-Lalande.

Though rooted in French soil, this wine has seen such brilliant success that one might ask if it has become a universal legacy, which begs the question, "Aren't these *grands crus* too costly, and reserved for a privileged few?" We recall that it takes two forty year-old plants to produce just 75 centiliters (25 fluid oz.) of a great Pichon wine. These grand old vintages – the grapes' quintessence – are not ordinary products; tasting them should be an experience. Other wines, like a *second vin* from Pichon, may accompany the everyday. But this question raises another one.

During the Terror, Lavoisier, the founder of modern chemistry, asked for one night's clemency before he was guillotined, so that he could write down the results of his last research. He was told, "The Republic does not need learned men!" Château Lafite, the Médoc's great star, was requisitioned during the Revolutionary era to make wine for the soldiers, and Pichon was nearly subjected to the same fate, yet one somehow doubts that the Republic needed *grands crus*, either. *Terroirs* like the Médoc are extraordinarily rare on this earth. Should they be reduced to producing table wines? Should they be punished for their excellence? One might as well ask that Rembrandt confine himself to engravings for peddlers, that Monet use his talent for newspaper caricatures, that Mozart compose circus music, that Victor Hugo write advertising copy.

Taste a Pichon-Lalande 1986, with its balance like a fine, taut silk on the tongue. It ends on a delicate, far-off coppery note, something pointed, sharp, like the faint call of a trumpet; you cannot ask man to abandon this embodiment of continuous perfectibility. It is inscribed in our very humanness. Tasted a year later, the same wine is almost unreal, with less weight in the mouth, so light and delicate you might be drinking in a dream. Move to a 1988 opened in 2005; it is smooth and deep, caressing you like a beloved woman. The 1986 is like a glimpse into the infinite; it invites meditation, introspection. Happiness wells through us, bringing new ideas, new resolutions, the urge to move ever further forward.

PICHON-LONGUEVILLE FAMILY TREE

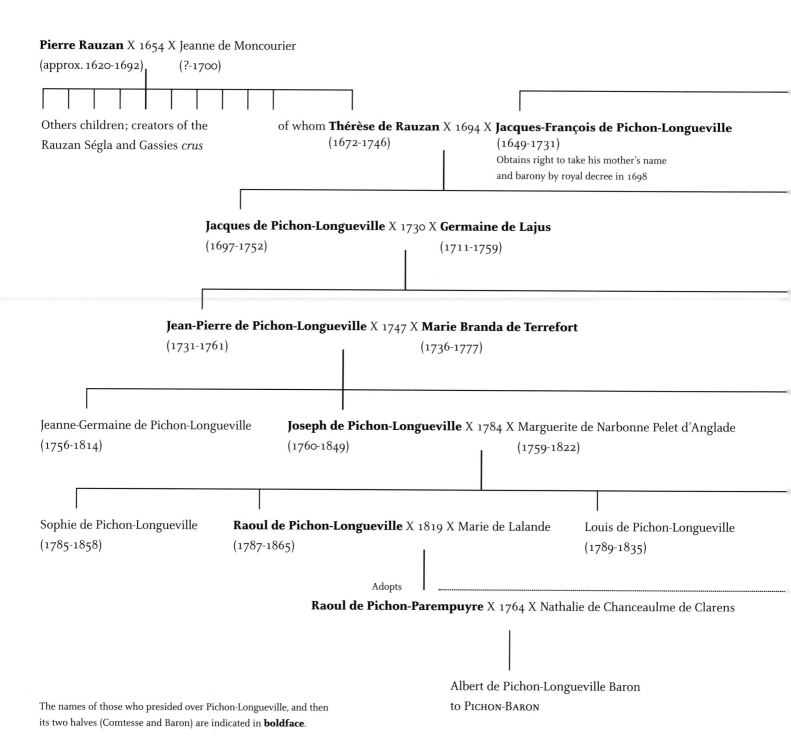

Pierre Rauzan X 1654 X Jeanne de Moncourier
(approx. 1620-1692)   (?-1700)

Others children; creators of the
Rauzan Ségla and Gassies *crus*

of whom **Thérèse de Rauzan** X 1694 X **Jacques-François de Pichon-Longueville**
(1672-1746)   (1649-1731)
Obtains right to take his mother's name
and barony by royal decree in 1698

Jacques de Pichon-Longueville X 1730 X **Germaine de Lajus**
(1697-1752)   (1711-1759)

Jean-Pierre de Pichon-Longueville X 1747 X **Marie Branda de Terrefort**
(1731-1761)   (1736-1777)

Jeanne-Germaine de Pichon-Longueville
(1756-1814)

Joseph de Pichon-Longueville X 1784 X Marguerite de Narbonne Pelet d'Anglade
(1760-1849)   (1759-1822)

Sophie de Pichon-Longueville
(1785-1858)

Raoul de Pichon-Longueville X 1819 X Marie de Lalande
(1787-1865)

Louis de Pichon-Longueville
(1789-1835)

Adopts

Raoul de Pichon-Parempuyre X 1764 X Nathalie de Chanceaulme de Clarens

Albert de Pichon-Longueville Baron
to PICHON-BARON

The names of those who presided over Pichon-Longueville, and then
its two halves (Comtesse and Baron) are indicated in **boldface**.

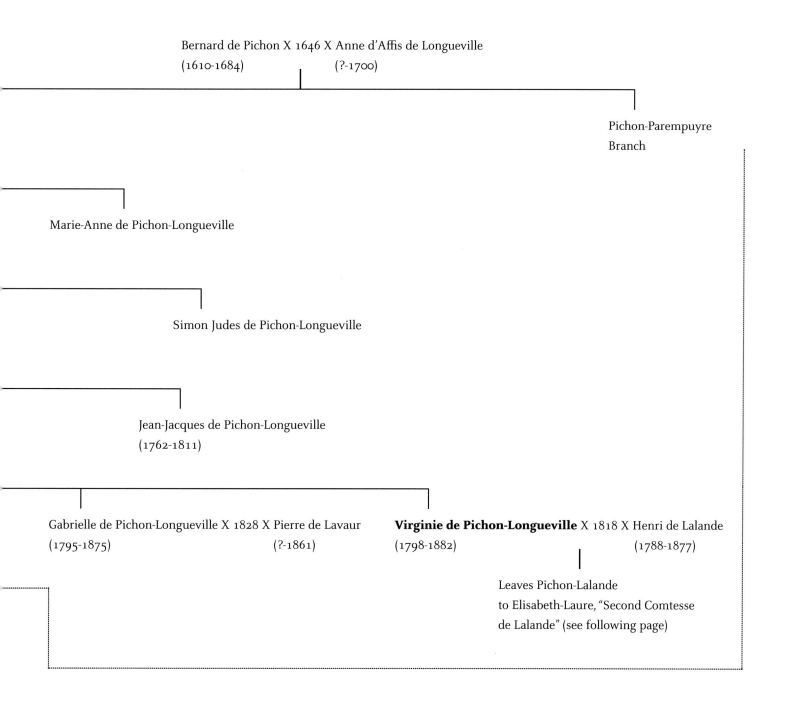

Bernard de Pichon X 1646 X Anne d'Affis de Longueville
(1610-1684)   (?-1700)

Pichon-Parempuyre
Branch

Marie-Anne de Pichon-Longueville

Simon Judes de Pichon-Longueville

Jean-Jacques de Pichon-Longueville
(1762-1811)

Gabrielle de Pichon-Longueville X 1828 X Pierre de Lavaur
(1795-1875)   (?-1861)

Virginie de Pichon-Longueville X 1818 X Henri de Lalande
(1798-1882)   (1788-1877)

Leaves Pichon-Lalande
to Elisabeth-Laure, "Second Comtesse
de Lalande" (see following page)

LALANDE AND LACROIX
FAMILY TREE

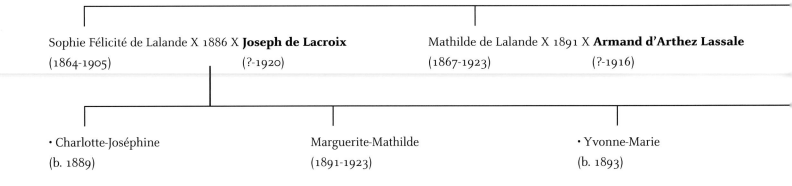

Sophie Félicité de Lalande X 1886 X **Joseph de Lacroix**
(1864-1905)   (?-1920)

Mathilde de Lalande X 1891 X **Armand d'Arthez Lassale**
(1867-1923)   (?-1916)

• Charlotte-Joséphine
(b. 1889)

Marguerite-Mathilde
(1891-1923)

• Yvonne-Marie
(b. 1893)

In 1925, Henriette-Marie de Lalande and the Lacroix heirs (Charlotte, Yvonne, Guy, Paul, and Raymond)
sold the Château de Lalande to Louis Miailhe and his shareholders' company.
Following the bankruptcy of a shareholder, Edouard Miailhe joined the company,
bringing the two brothers' share in the company to 55%.

The names of those who presided over Pichon-Lalande are indicated in **boldface**.
• Owners of the Château at the time of its sale to Louis Miailhe.

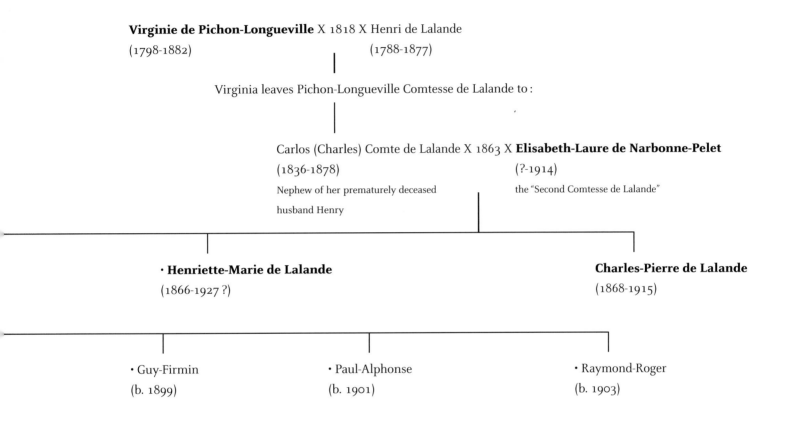

Virginie de Pichon-Longueville X 1818 X Henri de Lalande

(1798-1882)   (1788-1877)

Virginia leaves Pichon-Longueville Comtesse de Lalande to :

Carlos (Charles) Comte de Lalande X 1863 X **Elisabeth-Laure de Narbonne-Pelet**

(1836-1878)   (?-1914)

Nephew of her prematurely deceased   the "Second Comtesse de Lalande"

husband Henry

· **Henriette-Marie de Lalande**   **Charles-Pierre de Lalande**

(1866-1927 ?)   (1868-1915)

· Guy-Firmin   · Paul-Alphonse   · Raymond-Roger

(b. 1899)   (b. 1901)   (b. 1903)

THE MIAILHES:
A GREAT BORDEAUX WINE FAMILY

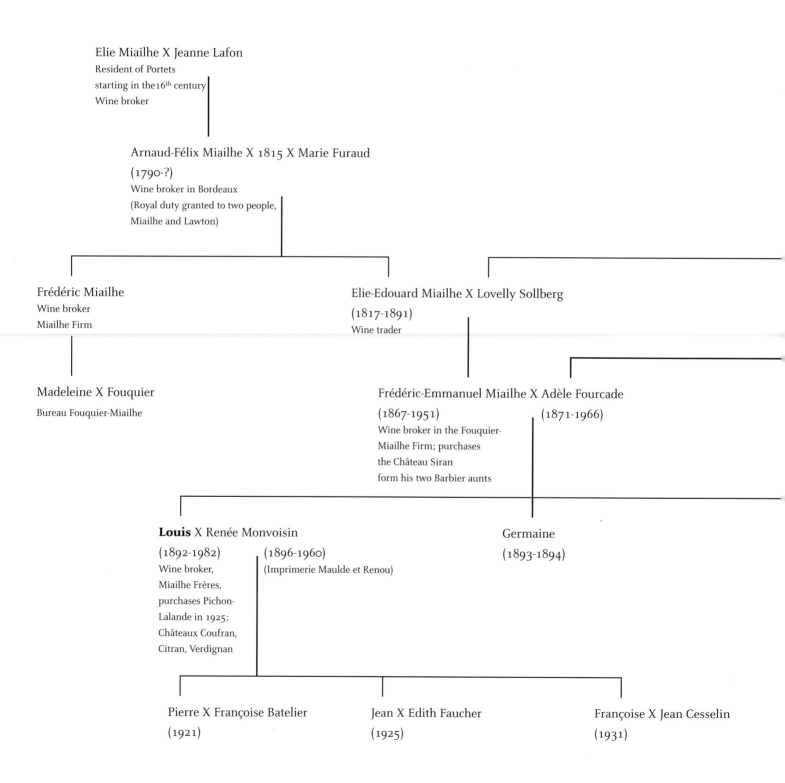

Elie Miailhe X Jeanne Lafon
Resident of Portets
starting in the16th century
Wine broker

Arnaud-Félix Miailhe X 1815 X Marie Furaud
(1790-?)
Wine broker in Bordeaux
(Royal duty granted to two people,
Miailhe and Lawton)

Frédéric Miailhe
Wine broker
Miailhe Firm

Elie-Edouard Miailhe X Lovelly Sollberg
(1817-1891)
Wine trader

Madeleine X Fouquier
Bureau Fouquier-Miailhe

Frédéric-Emmanuel Miailhe X Adèle Fourcade
(1867-1951)   (1871-1966)
Wine broker in the Fouquier-
Miailhe Firm; purchases
the Château Siran
form his two Barbier aunts

Louis X Renée Monvoisin
(1892-1982)   (1896-1960)
Wine broker,   (Imprimerie Maulde et Renou)
Miailhe Frères,
purchases Pichon-
Lalande in 1925;
Châteaux Coufran,
Citran, Verdignan

Germaine
(1893-1894)

Pierre X Françoise Batelier
(1921)

Jean X Edith Faucher
(1925)

Françoise X Jean Cesselin
(1931)

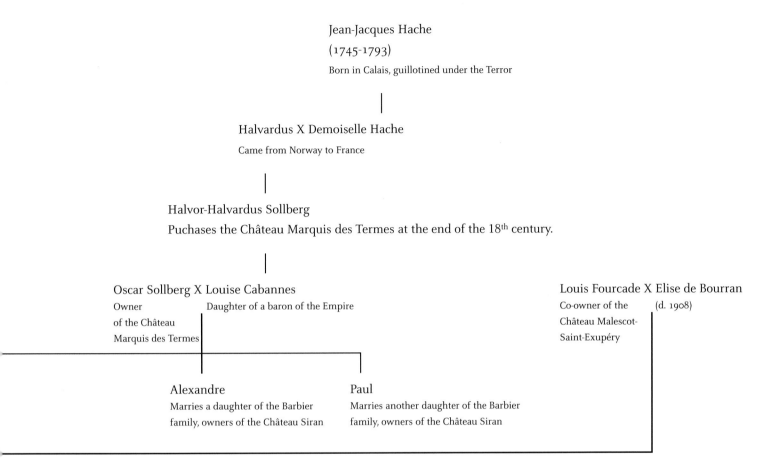

Jean-Jacques Hache
(1745-1793)
Born in Calais, guillotined under the Terror

Halvardus X Demoiselle Hache
Came from Norway to France

Halvor-Halvardus Sollberg
Puchases the Château Marquis des Termes at the end of the 18th century.

Oscar Sollberg X Louise Cabannes
Owner   Daughter of a baron of the Empire
of the Château
Marquis des Termes

Louis Fourcade X Elise de Bourran
Co-owner of the   (d. 1908)
Château Malescot-
Saint-Exupéry

Alexandre
Marries a daughter of the Barbier
family, owners of the Château Siran

Paul
Marries another daughter of the Barbier
family, owners of the Château Siran

Edouard
Wine broker, enters shareholders' company
Owner of Pichon-Lalande, which he directed
with his brother until 1959.
(see following page)

The name Miailhe comes from the Languedoc, from the Medieval Occitan word "mealha", which means "denier," a kind of coin.

Descendants of Edouard Miailhe and Anglo-Philippine ancestry of his wife, Victoria Desbarats

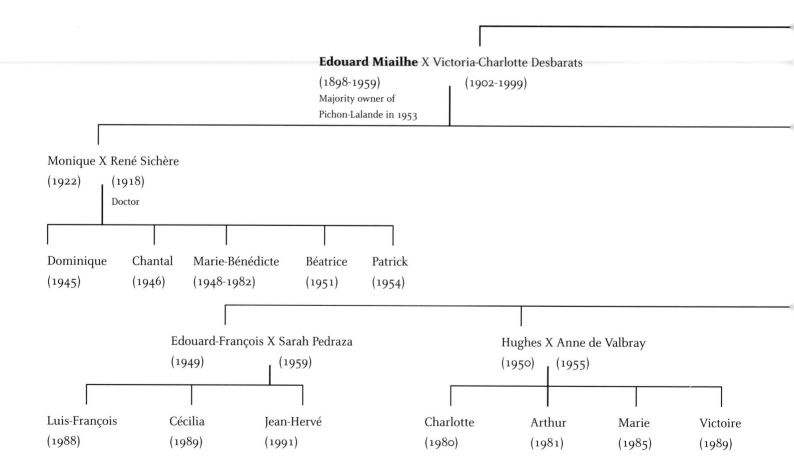

Edouard Miailhe X Victoria-Charlotte Desbarats

(1898-1959) (1902-1999)

Majority owner of
Pichon-Lalande in 1953

Monique X René Sichère

(1922) (1918)

Doctor

Dominique   Chantal   Marie-Bénédicte   Béatrice   Patrick

(1945)   (1946)   (1948-1982)   (1951)   (1954)

Edouard-François X Sarah Pedraza

(1949) (1959)

Hughes X Anne de Valbray

(1950) (1955)

Luis-François   Cécilia   Jean-Hervé

(1988)   (1989)   (1991)

Charlotte   Arthur   Marie   Victoire

(1980)   (1981)   (1985)   (1989)

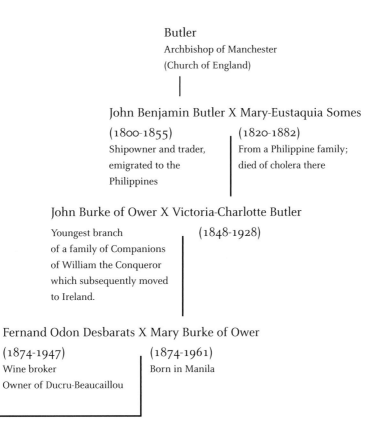

Butler
Archbishop of Manchester
(Church of England)

John Benjamin Butler X Mary-Eustaquia Somes

(1800-1855)
Shipowner and trader,
emigrated to the
Philippines

(1820-1882)
From a Philippine family;
died of cholera there

John Burke of Ower X Victoria-Charlotte Butler

Youngest branch
of a family of Companions
of William the Conqueror
which subsequently moved
to Ireland.

(1848-1928)

Fernand Odon Desbarats X Mary Burke of Ower

(1874-1947)
Wine broker
Owner of Ducru-Beaucaillou

(1874-1961)
Born in Manila

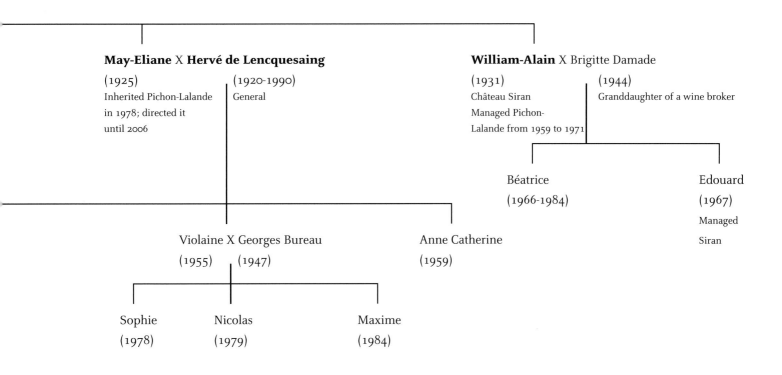

May-Eliane X **Hervé de Lencquesaing**

(1925)
Inherited Pichon-Lalande
in 1978; directed it
until 2006

(1920-1990)
General

William-Alain X Brigitte Damade

(1931)
Château Siran
Managed Pichon-
Lalande from 1959 to 1971

(1944)
Granddaughter of a wine broker

Béatrice
(1966-1984)

Edouard
(1967)
Managed
Siran

Violaine X Georges Bureau

(1955) (1947)

Anne Catherine
(1959)

Sophie
(1978)

Nicolas
(1979)

Maxime
(1984)

Pichon-Longueville Comtesse de Lalande Tasting notes

by Serena Sutcliffe

• 1916
Beautiful spiciness on the nose. Sharper than the '17. Coffee-ish.

• 1917
Beautiful scent. Lovely fruity silkiness. Lots of ripeness. So lingering. Incredible. Do not miss this if the opportunity arises.

• 1922
Lovely cedary scent. Tangerines (dried skins) on the palate.

• 1926
Glorious scent. Lacy and haunting. Great sweet aromatics. Soft, sweet, fragrant, classic vanilla pod old wine. Concentration and harmony. This remains a high point of the vintage. Another bottle reiterated the vanilla pod, liquid coffee and cinnamon character. Most recently, riveting, sweet, flower petals, complex nose. Extraordinary length and concentration. Ageing, but so lingering and fascinating on the palate.

• 1928
Excellent, classic, pure Pauillac bouquet. Sweet walnuts and raw beef on the palate. Sweet smoky coffee. This is a great 1928.

• 1929
The nose is old and cedary, but so intense. All the breed and elegance of '29. Pure mahogany with the sweetness of the vintage. A bit chocolate, and now a bit volatile. But wonderful.

• 1934
Lovely smoky, complex nose. Sweet and smoky on the palate. Chocolate-covered coffee bean finish. This was a year that had quality and quantity. Recently, complex, intense, intensely nostalgic nose. A mite volatile. Very intense on the palate, full of the breed of its terroir. A touch of aniseed at the end.

• 1937
Sweet, aniseed nose. Meaty. Finesse of texture. Really silky. This is excellent wine.

• 1938
Lovely sweet, blackcurrant nose. Really good for the year. Meaty and sweet. Great fruit.

• 1942
Glorious, nostalgic, rich nose. Great, great wine. So constant, so true, so rich. Everything in place. Amazing.

• 1945
Thick, dense colour. Riveting bouquet, unlike no other. Only '45s, and perhaps '61s, have that highly individualistic impact. Mega-rich, almost toffee nose. Sweetness and tar, coffee liqueur. Heather treacle! Great freshness and depth. Intense cassis taste with thick chocolate. So rich that any volatility is masked. Like a wonderfully exotic, exciting syrup. And the exuberance of this wine!

One of the greatest bottles of 1945 l have ever had. Beefy aftertaste. If all meat bouillons were like this!

A magnum had a lovely sweet, rich, concentrated nose. Rich and generous on the palate. Beefy and exuberant. Sweet and sassy. Most recently, it had an unbelievable intensity of bouquet and vintage on the nose. Sweet leather (almost American oak!). You look into the very heart of a wine with this. Huge concentration on the vine produced 1945. Massive, meaty character.

• 1947
A lovely sweet aniseed nose. Mouth-coating. Prune compote. Very exciting and exotic.

• 1948
A bit volatile on the nose. Very fruity and meaty on the palate. Lots of freshness. Solid.

• 1949
Vanilla with a touch of volatility on the nose. But also that Pichon scent. The volatility gives some acid on the palate but there is also inky, "iodé" fruit. Finesse of texture which is a hallmark of the 1949s.

• 1953
Warm chocolate and cocoa on the nose. So sweet. Thick, dense and ripe. Glorious smooth fruit. Solid for a '53. A great Pichon Lalande. Recently, shy, timid, ultrabeautiful nase. Enormous breed and finesse. So stunning, but seize it now. Succulent. A second bottle was fabulous. Great smoky complexity. So luscious. Divine.

• 1955
Slightly minty nose – Joe Heitz goes to Pauillac!* Sweet and meaty at the same time. Lovely sweet finish. Recently, great, concentrated red cherries nose. The acidity of '55 and such extraordinary red cherry taste. You don't get a long finish, but you get great attack.

• 1957
Warm liqueur nose. Essence of cedar and walnuts.

Soft tannins now.

• 1958
Lovely sweet nose. Such charm and delicacy. Amazing for the year.

• 1959
Great scent. A bouquet of roses, violets and smoke. Pure bliss. Such finesse, fruit and pure allure. This was the last vintage of May-Eliane de Lencquesaing's father and it is a lasting monument to him. The most recent bottle had the greatest, complex, fascinating nose. Utter refinement, utter breed. So soft it caresses the palate. Layers of taste. Pure nobility. St. Julien mixed with Pauillac.

• 1961
A completely different animal to the 1959. High alcohol. "Iodé". Blackcurrant leaves nose. Endless on the palate. The volume of the wine is impressive. Tar. The richness and the structure are amazing. The Power and the Glory. Lasts better in the glass than the magical 1959.

• 1962
At 44 years old, this has a glorious, sweet, cedary Pauillac bouquet. Sweet, meaty and fabulous on the palate. So succulent. *Un rêve.*

• 1964
Such a ripe, sweet nose. Aniseed. The taste is "sweet" too. Really lovely. Such finesse and sweetness. Filigree lace. Recently, a marvellous gamey nose. Sweet aniseed. Fascinating and intriguing. The aniseed bouquet is amazing. Just melts on the palate. The most perfect mature claret.

• 1966
Wonderful, cedary nose. Such elegance and flavour. Perfect "now" drinking.

* Ms Sutcliffe is referring to the celebrated California winemaker Joe Heitz, now deceased.

• 1967
Spicy nose. Now a bit volatile, but pruney finish.

• 1970
Immensely aromatic with all the dry, oriental spices, as they hover in the warmth of the Tropics! As the wine airs, the meatiness emerges. Huge impact of prunes and dried fruit on the palate. But the finish is still so fresh. Cinnamon sticks and brown sugar. On this showing, approaching its apogee.

• 1971
Mature cedarwood nose of charm. Liqueur finish. Cocoa. Walnut liqueur.

• 1975
Michel Delon made this for the owning family. Chocolatey and thick with a sweet, ripe finish. All the tannin has softened. A recent bottle had an extremely scented nose. Maraschino cherries. Succulent and sweet taste. And the Pichon finesse. Both chocolatey and meaty. This has to be right at the top of the 1975's now.

• 1978
So aromatic and classy and so "top cru". Such coffee tastes. Lovely and spicy. Drink now. Rich and unctuous. Recently, a wonderful Cabernet nose. Deep, intense and aromatic. Like crunching blackcurrants. A great, late-vintage wine.

• 1979
Very scented and violetty. So full and plummy in the mouth. Delicious fruit. So healthy and pure. Finish of cold coffee. One senses the St. Julien part of the vineyard here.

• 1980
Aromatic nose – very Cabernet. Good fruit on the middle palate. Short now, but clean.

• 1981
This has great freshness and cedary quality. So bouncy and vivacious. So elegant and seamless.

• 1982
A bouquet of such class and breed. In the mouth, you almost eat it. Glorious spice bazaar taste. Chocolate and cinnamon plus blackberry compote. Freshness and density, a great combination. Recently, a great, sweet leather nose and great "raisins de Corinthe", curranty taste. Is this stunning wine going back to its exotic origins after going through a "classic" period? It does not matter – it is simply marvellous!

• 1983
Such a heavenly, chocolate and violets nose. Glorious velvet curtains on the palate. Wonderful red cherries. All-enveloping. Cloves at the end, with the freshness of the Petit Verdot. This is a superb wine and a terrific 1983. Another bottle had an incredibly spicy nose of enormous ripeness. Magnificent, deep velvet wine. All-enveloping, super-flavoury, just oozing fruit and succulence. What astonishes in this now variable year is the extraordinary generosity of the wine. There is no other 1983 l enjoy drinking more.

• 1984
So warm and spicy on the nose. Such freshness. A touch of Seville oranges. Very good for the year, the result of enormous selection.

• 1985
Glorious macerated cherries on the nose. So opulent, so fat and such charm. Lovely texture. So silky and seductive. (From double magnum, a heavenly great violets nose. The taste is extra deep in this format.) Recently, extraordinary, blackberry opulence. The absolute beauty of great MerIot. So complete. The room is always divided on this versus the 1986 – 1 adore them both.

• 1986
Very aromatic and very cedary on the nose. So scented. Very Cabernet. Cassis and blackbenies. So smooth and

classic. Recently, great complexity and Cabernet Sauvignon aromatics. Enormous, intense, multi-dimensional bouquet. Sweet, long, glycerol taste. Great "legs". Richness. This has a long life in front of it.

• 1987
Sweet, fruity nose. Lots of sweet, fresh fruit on the palate. Just slips down.

• 1988
Classically cedary and a great Pauillac nose. So clean and defined. Pure fruit and perfect structure. The '88 is classic Bordeaux.

• 1989
Such a classy nose of real breed and ripeness. Such freshness, with huge fruit and fat covering the tannic structure. Very Merlot finish. Superb. It is sa exotic but is it becoming more classic? Recently, a hot, melting nose, with the strong vintage character overriding the Pichon Lalande character. Sweet and pure coffee and cocoa on the palate. Coffee beans plus all the oriental spices. So full of texture you can eat it.

• 1990
Lovely "sweet", violetty nose. So sweet and ripe on the palate. No huge structure, but so silky and attractive. Another bottle had a spicy, cinnamon nose. Woodsmoke and coffee. Very exotic and oriental. On the light side, but delicious. Quite an irony finish. And meltingly soft on the palate.

• 1991
The real bouquet of a grand vin. Deep, aromatically intense (the mark of those few excellent 1991s, all on the best terroirs) – like spiced hot chocolate! Blackcurrant comes through. Almost smoky. Wonderful fruit in the middle. Damsons and a touch of prunes. The finish is not megalong, so it is perfect drinking now and for the next 10 years. A remarkable achievement*. Aftertaste of roast lamb and redcurrant jelly. Try the wine against the real thing!

• 1992
Pretty, cedary scent. Light, meaty taste. Touch of bitter espresso. Very quaffable but drink now.

• 1993
Rosy, violetty scent, typical of the best Pauillac properties in this year. Lots of pretty fruit. A touch herbaceous on the finish. Aftertaste of prunes and vanilla pod.

• 1994
Lovely spicy nose. Lovely meaty attack. Delicious and velvety. A real miracle in the year, with no dryness.

• 1995
Very Merlot, plummy, even St. Emilion nose! Luscious, opulent taste, without the huge complexity of 1996 – more straightforward. One-dimensional, but what a dimension! Chocolate finish. Recently, so blueberry, such a bilberry nose. Absolutely blooms. Massively Merlot. Musky, coffee-ish and huge black fruit. Less complex than the '96 but a humdinger.

• 1996
Glorious, winning aromatic bouquet of a top vintage. Stunning damson taste. Drenched in intense fruit. The base of great concentrated Petit Verdot. Cassis and walnuts at the end. Recently, pure Cabernet beauty. Utterly luscious, a total A1 wine. The glycerol to match the structure – immense fruit. It has everything. Great richness surrounds the power.

• 1997
Lovely freshness and fruit. Really good. Just melts in the mouth.

• 1998
Really classy scent. Very beautiful, refined fruit, backed up by real depth. Classy all the way through. More

* A reference to the terrible spring frosts which devastated the Médoc that year.

recently, there was beautiful oak and fruit on the nose. Very aromatic. Such a "meaty" wine. Four square. Big and structured. Chewy finish.

• 1999

Great class on the nose. Scent and breed. Lovely chocolate tastes. Layers of fruit and all the finesse of the cru. Very good indeed.

• 2000

This is a vintage where picking continued until 9th October.
Extraordinary health of fruit. Such aromas, so primary, so glorious. Huge tannin. So plummy, although it is a Cabernet Sauvignon and Petit Verdot (10%) year. Great red fruit and such freshness. Recently, like a glühwein on the nose – so aromatic and intoxicating. Cocoa, spices, richness and glycerol. Fabulous – like a liqueur. It just gets better and better.

• 2001

An amazing 14% Petit Verdot in this. Lovely, pure, keen cassis nose. Great breed and enormous scent. Glorious mocha and glycerol, with tremendous purity and line. So well-bred and with such a fine texture.

• 2002

The oak is still very present at this stage but all the balance and harmony of Pichon Lalande is there. Knitting together very well.

• 2003

Fascinating mineral elements on the nose. Incredibly intense and full. Sparking on all cylinders. This is turning into a star of this starry vintage.

• 2004

Classy nose, deep berry fruit on the palate. Highly successful.

BIBLIOGRAPHY

Below we have noted the key works consulted, starting with those that cover Pichon-Longueville's beginnings to 1850, and followed by documents on Pichon-Longueville Lalande up to the present day.

Pichon-Longueville Comtesse de Lalande château archives

These archives comprise several different sources. It is a rich collection, though it does favor some periods over others.

Our first sources come from documents belonging to the Pichon-Longueville family, and contain numerous items pertaining to the family and property. Virginie de Lalande most likely took these original documents to the château during its construction or after the deaths of her brother Raoul and her sister Gabrielle. We were told that the Pichon-Longueville Baron archives had all been either destroyed or sold off over the last century. It would seem, then, that Pichon-Longueville Comtesse holds all record of the two vineyards before 1850. The documents were hidden away in one of the château's attics until Madame de Lencquesaing discovered and archived them.

Information starting with the chapter entitled "The Age of Crisis and Disease" comes from a second set of sources. It spans 40 years, beginning after Virginie's death and ending with the sale of the château to Louis Miailhe and his company. Sources from the Lalande and Lacroix periods provide much documentation about the property, but less about the owners themselves. These sources are:

• A collection of log books kept by the estate stewards, including Gabriel Vigneaux. Though these records grow increasingly incomplete after 1914, they note daily in and in detail the winegrowing and winemaking operations undertaken at Pichon-Lalande from 1883 to 1920, including day-to-day meteorological observations, quantities of grapes harvested in each vintage, and different vine treatments. This trove of fascinating information, which dates from the era of phylloxera and mildew, traces day by day the origins of the exceptional 1893 vintage, harvested in mid-August in temperatures reaching 46°C (115°F).

• Letters from the owners to Gabriel Vigneaux, Pichon-Lalande's estate steward, dating from 1904 to 1907. Sent mainly from Bayonne, Paris, and Perpignan, they reveal much about Pichon-Lalande's situation during these difficult years. Several telegrams are included in this correspondence as well.

• Documentation for this period also includes various invoices addressed to Vigneaux and his successor, Champagne.

Our third set of sources covers the Miailhe years:
• A set of invoices dated from 1925 to 1959, the year of Edouard Miailhe's death and of Louis's retirement.
• A 1934 insurance company appraisal of the château and all its contents, which was updated in 1938 and again in 1941.
• Numerous bills of sale for wine in casks (and sometimes in bottles) from 1926 to 1957.
• Significant photographic archives concerning the Miailhe family and its Cours de la Martinique offices.

The de Lencquesaing period is of course the richest (even disproportionately so) source of written and pictorial documentation, which has been stored at the château ever since May-Eliane and Hervé de Lencquesaing took it over in May 1978.

Tastet-Lawton brokerage office archives

The Lawtons need no introduction in the Médoc. Arrived in France from Cork, Ireland, in 1718, they recall those Egyptian scribes who recorded the fate of each and every rock they saw, from its origin in the quarry to its final resting place in a pyramid or temple. For three centuries, from Abraham to Daniel Lawton, they were not only leading brokers, but also acted as notaries, or *notaries*, for the great Médoc wines. Their logs, kept in legible, elegant script, are moving to read – like writing in its Platonic form. Studying the Lawtons' logbooks, one cannot help but think that writing was invented for such clarity, for enumerating the wealth brought forth from the earth.

We would like to extend our warmest thanks to Daniel Lawton, who helped us review the extensive figures he had available. Along with the data we found at Pichon-Lalande, it allowed us to verify our hypotheses, round out our information, and cast new light on many of our questions.

Works consulted

We have cited in alphabetical order those works which had the most influence on our research. For the sake of conciseness, we avoided listing general works on the Revolution or works very particular to Bordeaux of the period. For these we refer the reader to the appendix of our novel *Le vin de la Liberté*.

Bluche, F. *Dictionnaire du Grand Siècle*. Paris: Fayard, 1990.

Boscheron des Portes, C.-B.-F. *Histoire du Parlement de Bordeaux depuis sa création jusqu'à sa suppression (1451-1790)*. 2 vols. Bordeaux: Lefebvre, 1877.

Devienne, Dom. *Histoire de la ville de Bordeaux*. Bordeaux: de la Court fils, 1771.

Etienne, R., ed. *Histoire de Bordeaux*. Toulouse: Privat, 1990.

Figeac, M. *Destins de la noblesse bordelaise (1770-1830)*. Bordeaux: Fédération historique du Sud-Ouest, 1996.

Higounet, C., ed.
• *Histoire de Bordeaux*. 7 vols. Bordeaux: Fédération historique du Sud-Ouest, 1962-1972.
• *Histoire de l'Aquitaine*. Toulouse: Privat, 1971.
• *La seigneurie et le vignoble de Château Latour:*

Histoire d'un grand cru du Médoc (XIVe-XXe siècle).
Bordeaux: Fédération historique du Sud-Ouest, 1974.
Huetz de Lemps, C. *Géographie du commerce
de Bordeaux à la fin du règne de Louis XIV.* Paris:
Éditions de l'EHESS, 1975.

Kellein, T. *Caspar David Friedrich, Der künstlerische
Weg.* Munich: Prestel, 1998.

de Lencquesaing, E.-F. *Général Hervé de Lencquesaing,
L'héroïsme discret d'une époque.* Paris: Éditions du Félin,
2002.

Lever, E. *Louis XVIII.* Paris: Fayard, 1988.

Markham Jr., D. 1855, *Histoire d'un Classement des vins
de Bordeaux.* Bordeaux: Féret & Fils, 1997.

Moretti, V. *Le più belle del reale.* Rome: Nova Spada
Editore, 1983. (Study of female painters in history,
particularly female self-portraiture through the ages.)

Pees, J. "Les Pichon-Longueville, un nom, un patrimoine,
à travers un siècle d'histoire, 1750-1850," history thesis,
under the direction of Philippe Loupes and Michel
Figeac, Université Bordeaux III, Michel Montaigne,
Institut d'histoire, 1998.

Pernot, M. *La Fronde.* Paris: Éditions de Fallois, 1994.

Pianzola, M. *Paysages romantiques genevois.* Geneva:
Musée d'art et d'histoire, 1977.

Pijassou, R.
• *Le Médoc, Un grand vignoble de qualité.* Paris:
Tallandier, 1980.

• *Château Rauzan-Ségla.* Paris:
Éditions de La Martinière, 2004.
Ranum, O. *La Fronde.* L'Univers historique. Paris:
Le Seuil, 1995.

J. Tulard,
• *Les Vingt Jours, 1er-20 mars 1815.* Paris: Fayard, 2001.
• ed. Dictionnaire Napoléon. Paris: Fayard, 1989.

ACKNOWLEDGEMENTS

First, I would like to thank May-Eliane de Lencquesaing, who wanted this book, who entrusted me with the writing of it, and who participated in its creation by contributing her own memories to it, deeply intertwined as they are with the history of 20th century Médoc. Without her tireless effort in building its archives and collecting and restoring the far flung elements of this story – with the help of General Hervé de Lencquesaing, who went all the way to Germany to uncover Sophie's past – the memory of Pichon-Longueville Comtesse de Lalande would no doubt have faded away. I would also like to thank Marie-Chantal Leboucq, who provided vital documentation and contacts. This work could never have been done without the constant support of the team at the château. The people who contribute on a daily basis to the making of the wine generously gave me all manner of help, detail, contact information, and encouragement. I thank managing director Gildas d'Ollone, financial director Jean-Claude Lafrance, and technical director Thomas Dô-Chi-Nam. Among the secretarial staff, I am particularly grateful to Christine Renassia for her tireless aid and humor, and to Fabienne Durou for her help in the archives, particularly with the Lalande family, on which she had done much work. My thanks also to Karine Pieuchot, Astrid Guillaume, Danielle Sigalat, Sylvie Beheretche-Gasqueton, Xavier Pallu, Marc and Laurence Noury, Violette Peigne, Laurent Maurin, and many others who so kindly offered their help in this project.

I am very grateful to Edouard, Hughes, Violaine, and Anne Catherine de Lencquesaing for their memories of their father, General de Lencquesaing, about whom Edouard has written a book, and for their encouragement and ideas.

Many thanks to Serena Sutcliffe, who gave permission to reproduce her tasting notes, and who wrote the preface to this book.

Dominique Sichère gave me the necessary information for the Miailhe family tree; Maylis Sichère-Lawton answered my legal questions about inheritance after the Revolution; Daniel Lawton provided access to the books and archives of the celebrated Tastet-Lawton brokerage; I am very grateful to them all. I thank Laure Vernière for her support and judicious commentary, and Françoise du Sorbier, who kindly proofread my translation of Serena Sutcliffe's tasting notes.

I am thankful to Robert Assaf both for his encouragement and for his thoughtful reading, and for furnishing the English translation of this book through his company, Corporate Editions, where Miranda Richmond-Mouillot and Jennifer Cohen translated, aided by Elizabeth Washburn.

I am indebted to the work of René Pijassou, who wrote several books on the Médoc, which have become classics in the field, and to Johanna Pees' history thesis. It was Mr. Pijassou who drew my attention to the crucial question of the sulfured wick during our meeting at Cos d'Estournel. Caroline le Mao and Michel Figeac, who directed Johanna Pees' thesis, provided important information about Bernard de Pichon over lunch at the château. I am very grateful to them all.

I would like to thank everyone at Éditions de La Martinière, including Corinne Schmidt and Nathalie Mayevski, as well as graphic designer Lorette Mayon. They unstintingly offered their time and their talent to this book.

Finally, I would like to remember two people who are no longer with us. Katherine Haziot read the first part of this book and offered me endless encouragement. Florentina Gallardo, known as Tata, took care of me during my long stays over holidays, when I worked alone at the comtesse's château, surrounded by portraits of the people I was charged with bringing to life.

PHOTOGRAPHIC CREDITS

First published by Éditions La Martinière, Paris, 2007

Copyright © 2007 Éditions de La Martinière, an imprint of La Martinière Groupe, Paris

Distributed in North America by Stewart, Tabori & Chang
An imprint of Harry N. Abrams, Inc.

ISBN: 978-1-58479-724-1

Printed and bound in France

HNA ▌▌▌▌▌
harry n. abrams, inc.
a subsidiary of La Martinière Groupe

115 West 18th Street
New York, NY 10011
www.hnabooks.com